GHOSTS, GANGSTERS AND GAMBLERS OF LAS VEGAS

WELCOME TO *Fabulous* DOWNTOWN LAS VEGAS NEVADA

Liz Cavanaugh

Michelle Broussard Honick

Vernell Hackett

Schiffer Publishing Ltd®

4880 Lower Valley Road, Atglen, Pennsylvania 19310

Cover photo: Cacino and Limo © Photobeard. Photo courtesy of bigstockphotos.com.
Ouija is a registered trademark of Parker Brothers Games.
All photos unless otherwise noted are copyrighted by Author Liz Cavanaugh
Author photo depiction on back cover: Costumed characters courtesy of the A "Le" Inn

Schiffer Books are available at special discounts for bulk purchases for sales promotions
or premiums. Special editions, including personalized covers, corporate imprints, and
excerpts can be created in large quantities for special needs. For more information contact
the publisher:

Published by Schiffer Publishing Ltd.
4880 Lower Valley Road
Atglen, PA 19310
Phone: (610) 593-1777; Fax: (610) 593-2002
E-mail: Info@schifferbooks.com

For the largest selection of fine reference books on this and related subjects, please visit our
web site at **www.schifferbooks.com**
We are always looking for people to write books on new and related subjects. If you have an
idea for a book please contact us at the above address.

This book may be purchased from the publisher. Include $5.00 for shipping.
Please try your bookstore first. You may write for a free catalog.

In Europe, Schiffer books are distributed by
Bushwood Books
6 Marksbury Ave.
Kew Gardens
Surrey TW9 4JF England
Phone: 44 (0) 20 8392-8585; Fax: 44 (0) 20 8392-9876
E-mail: info@bushwoodbooks.co.uk
Website: www.bushwoodbooks.co.uk

Copyright © 2009 by Liz Cavanaugh, Michelle Broussard Honick, and Vernell Hackett
Library of Congress Control Number: 2009925583

Designed by Stephanie Daugherty
Type set in Rosemary Roman/New Baskerville BT

ISBN: 978-0-7643-3294-4
Printed in China

 2

CONTENTS

ACKNOWLEDGMENTS

We would like to thank the following people for their assistance and knowledge: Darin Hollingsworth, The Liberace Museum; John Hosier, Carluccio's Tivoli Gardens; Richard Reed, insidervlv.com; Robert Allen, Haunted Las Vegas Tours; Erin Pavlina; Shannon O'Day, and Paul Bordenkircher.

Special thanks also go to our family and friends who offered their love, support, and patience while we worked on the project.

And, as Bob Barker would say, please remember to spay and neuter your pets.

Introduction:

Ghosts, Gangsters, and a Few Good Gamblers

Forget the idea that ghosts only hang out in dark, scary places in the dead of night. The bright lights, jangling slot machines, and glittering shows of Las Vegas are the background for hauntings that prove that long-held myth just isn't necessarily so.

From the backstage corridor where the Righteous Brothers' Bobby Hatfield has been spotted walking to the last stage where he ever performed, to the park where specters of murdered children make their presence known, to the popular museum where Liberace still enjoys his piano and sparkling costumes, to the rose garden where Bugsy Siegel has been seen beside his own monument, to all the other sites of apparitions in Las Vegas, one can say Sin City truly is a haunted town.

Las Vegas is a place of extreme emotions—from the exhilaration of gambling and winning to the sometimes suicidal depression caused by losing. There are glamorous superstars performing nightly at fabulous showrooms, hard-working support staff that keeps the illusions going, and overwhelmed tourists who don't want to miss a thing. Anywhere with such strong emotions, 24/7 energy, and oversized personalities seems to be a natural magnet for spirits.

It's a city that's seen the control of gangsters, the almost unbelievable rise of hotel-casinos, the perhaps unprecedented growth of tourism, and the glamour of entertainers like the Rat Pack, Elvis, and Cirque de Soleil. It's witnessed the strangeness of Howard Hughes, the filming of major movies like *Ocean's Eleven,* and—most amazingly—the change from a tiny Western settlement to the acknowledged entertainment center of the world.

Remember, too, there also is a separate Vegas that doesn't have a thing to do with the excitement we think of as Sin City. It has its own crimes, disasters, and history, as does the area surrounding Vegas. There seems to be a very good reason, for instance, for deserted mining towns to be called ghost towns.

Las Vegas has changed spectacularly throughout its years of existence, but one thing that has remained the same is that many of its residents and visitors are reluctant to leave. Obviously, it sometimes is literally true that "What happens in Vegas stays in Vegas."

1

THE HISTORY
OF LAS VEGAS

L as Vegas has, from the start, been a city of gamblers. It's located just 150 miles from Death Valley in the Mojave Desert. Its four large freshwater springs and stream first attracted the Anasazi tribe beginning around 300 BC and later the Paiute Indians (also known as Diggers). When a Mexican trade caravan led by Antonio Armijo visited those springs in 1829, traveling on the Old Spanish Trail, its scout, Rafael Rivera, named the area of the springs Las Vegas, which means "the meadow" in Spanish.

The name stuck, even though not many settlers did. Mormon missionaries tried it in 1885, but left the settlement and fort they'd built only three years later. They had used it since it went along the trail which connected southern California to the Mormons' Salt Lake City headquarters. Miners who came to the area to search for tin, lead, and gold were transient instead of long-term settlers.

In 1900, a grand total of thirty people lived in the whole Las Vegas Valley. A few ranchers, especially those at O. D. Gass' Las Vegas Ranch and Farm complex (on the site of the old Mormon fort) and the Kyle (or Kiel) Ranch, hung around but even an oasis is still in the middle of a desert, after all. Who else but a gambler would actually believe a place like that could be a truly viable habitat, much less one of the most famous cities in the world?

The first big break was when Senator William Clark from Montana—one of those gamblers—decided that Vegas should be the site for the repairs for the San Pedro, Los Angeles & Salt Lake City Railroad (later called the Union Pacific) spur, which would connect the Transcontinental Railroad to southern California. Senator Clark went farther than that, though. He bought Helen Stewart's 2,000-acre cattle ranch and water rights, set up the Las Vegas Land and Water Company, planned a town to be located beside the railroad tracks, advertised free train fare for those buying tracts of his land (at the princely price of between $150-$750 per lot), and held an auction on May 15, 1905 for the rest of the sites. That date is considered the founding date for the city of Las Vegas. In a two-day sale, Clark's profit was almost five times what he'd paid for the land.

The railroad had been completed just a few months earlier, in January of 1905. A booming rival town site (eventually called the West Side) had been started about that time by J. T. McWilliams, but Clark's area, with its early tented town, quickly caused its decline. Clark's site became the center of Las Vegas. It became the county seat in 1908-1909, and the city was incorporated on March 16, 1911. It was the first city in Nevada to adopt a mayor/commissioners government.

Even then, Vegas had its wild side. Block 16 sported saloons, gambling houses, and prostitution to help the hard-working railroad men relax in their off-time. The town was bustling until over ten percent of the railroad workers lost their jobs in 1917. The situation got worse four years later when Union Pacific bought the railroad and cut sixty more jobs. The next year, workers went on strike. Businesses closed when their freight couldn't be unloaded from the trains, and Union Pacific vengefully moved its maintenance shop out of Vegas.

Lesser towns would have been destroyed, but not Las Vegas. Some dreamers wanted to turn it into a resort town even as early as the Roaring Twenties, but for the time being, its survival depended on things that were considered vices in other places—prizefighting (the only state where it was legal), saloons (open even during the Depression), and quick divorces (requiring only a six month, and later a three month, residence before the divorce was granted). Things were about to get a lot better for Vegas, though.

The construction of Boulder Dam (now known as the Hoover Dam), to be located only thirty miles southeast of Vegas, was authorized by President Calvin Coolidge. To become the largest dam in the world, it revitalized the area completely. It brought water from the Colorado River, electricity, and, perhaps just as importantly at that time, thousands of jobs. When construction on the dam began on September 7, 1929, so did a huge building boom in Vegas. All those workers needed places to live and eat as well as obtain all the other necessities and pleasures of life. Within a single year, the city's population grew by fifty percent. Night clubs (including the Red Rooster, the first on the area now called the Strip) and supper clubs (the first called The Meadows) opened and gambling locations increased because the dam builders couldn't gamble or drink liquor close to their worksite. They were close enough to Vegas to indulge their vices in the city.

The Vegas we know today had its beginning when Nevada became the first state to legalize casino gambling. The first casino license was issued to Mayme Stocker in 1920 for Fremont Street's Northern Club. Hotels with gambling casinos and showrooms with live entertainment first opened in Vegas in the early thirties. The Nevada Legislature passed a gambling bill in 1931 to raise taxes for public schools; almost a third of the annual state budget today is derived from the tax on casino winnings. With gambling legalized in Nevada, it brought a lot of tourism and tax dollars since it was outlawed in other states. The Gaming Control Board was begun in 1955, with the Nevada Gaming Commission created in 1959 to control gambling practices. Today, the hotels and casinos employ about 166,000 of Las Vegas' more than two million residents.

To further entice visitors, Nevada also legalized horse racing and reduced the residency requirement for divorce down to just six weeks. After the publicity when Ria Langham Gable moved to Vegas for the residency requirement for her divorce from movie legend Clark Gable, Vegas joined Reno in becoming the divorce capitals of America.

Conversely, Vegas later also became known as a wedding capital, offering 24-hour wedding chapels that issue from 87,000 to 120,000 marriage licenses every year. It also averages about 150 to 337 weddings each day. No waiting period or blood tests were required to obtain a marriage license there, which was attractive not only to drunken gamblers but also to celebrities (like Elvis and Priscilla Presley, Frank Sinatra and Mia Farrow, Bruce Willis and Demi Moore, Dennis Rodman and Carmen Electra, Mickey Rooney and Ava Gardner, Richard Gere and Cindy Crawford, Zsa Zsa Gabor and George Sanders, and Rita Hayworth and Dick Haymes, among others) wanting to avoid pre-wedding publicity or a lengthy waiting period.

Current chapels even feature Elvis impersonators and drive-through weddings. Theme weddings (Wild West, medieval, pirate, and Egyptian among them) are also popular in Vegas, as are more athletic type weddings (bungee jumping, skydiving or on a roller coaster). Only in Vegas.

For those without marriage on their minds, prostitution in Vegas is still illegal, though many efforts have been made throughout the years to legalize it in the city. Nevada law, however, still prohibits brothels in counties with more than 400,000 residents. The closest legal prostitution to Vegas is about sixty miles away in Nye County.

The Hoover Dam, which opened in Black Canyon in September of 1936, attracted a lot of visitors to the area. The Las Vegas Gunnery School (Nellis Air Force Base) also opened close to the city in 1941, as did Basic Magnesium Incorporated (manufacturer of metallic magnesium used in airplanes and during World War II in bombs, with a huge complex valued at $150 million). All of these combined to synergistically grow the area's economy, tourism industry, and population tremendously.

By 1938, former Los Angeles Police Department Captain Guy McAfee and his associates had taken over most of the casino business in Vegas. McAfee was the one who nicknamed Highway 91 "The Strip" when he opened his Pair o' Dice Club there. Thomas Hull also built his El Rancho Vegas resort hotel, featuring a showroom with beautiful chorus girls, on Highway 91. This was the precursor to the huge takeover by the mob starting with Ben Siegel's opening of the Flamingo Hotel & Casino. "The Boys" controlled Vegas' gambling casinos and took their profits off the top in the back counting rooms for decades.

At that time, casino owners by law had to be individually licensed, which worked out fine for the mobs, whose front men could be licensed with no problem. It wasn't until the mid-sixties that public companies with stockholders legally could become casino owners in Vegas. That created the ideal situation for a billionaire like Howard Hughes, whose companies took over multiple casinos in a buying frenzy starting in 1967. The state was particularly attractive to him since it had no state corporate tax, income tax, or inheritance tax. Hughes' purchase of the properties was equally attractive to Vegas because its reputation was boosted tremendously by such a high-profile, legitimate businessman taking over the formerly mob-owned hotel-casinos. Steve Wynn and Kirk Kerkorian continued this trend, and it ended up being a major factor in driving the mob out of Vegas and creating today's modern, elaborately themed casinos and resort hotels.

Helldorado Days, celebrating its Old West cowboy history with big parades, a rodeo, beard growing contests, cattle roping, and bronc riding, were a big deal in Vegas from 1935 into the fifties, when Vegas decided to upgrade to a more glamorous image.

About that time, Vegas became known as "Atomic City, U.S.A." Atom bomb tests first took place in the area on January 27, 1951, after which 120 bombs were detonated about sixty-five miles from Vegas over the next twelve years. The Nevada Proving Ground test site of the U. S. Atomic Energy Commission brought a strong military presence (hundreds of jobs, military assistance, and even more tourism) to Vegas, and the bomb tests were seen as both safe and even patriotic in the Cold War period. Hotel guests would view the detonations at "dawn bomb parties." There even were special atomic cocktails, atomic bomb picnic lunches (to take visitors closer to the site to watch the testing), atomic hairstyles, and a variety of atomic bomb souvenirs offered in Vegas.

This excitement, of course, all happened before the public became aware of the horrible results of radiation poisoning caused by the testing's fallout over southern Utah. Respected scientist Linus Pauling believed nuclear testing in the area caused leukemia in approximately 10,000 people. Written reports have said it may even have contributed to the development of fatal cancer in many of the actors (including John Wayne and Susan Hayward) who had filmed the movie *The Conqueror* about Genghis Khan close to the desert testing area in 1956.

An adjacent area, the Nuclear Rocket Development Station, opened in 1957 as a 90,000-acre test area for nuclear powered rockets. Besides the obvious defense uses, this was an important site for developing rockets for outer space, which America was just beginning to explore.

Vegas' own population tripled in the fifties to more than 127,000 inhabitants (including those in the suburbs). It had just 8,422 residents in the 1940 census.

After United Airlines began its jet service to Vegas in 1960, it became a huge convention city, offering inexpensive hotel rooms and free drinks, as well as enormous, cheap buffets throughout the day and night. Vegas, after all, was a city that didn't seem to sleep.

With Frank Sinatra's Rat Pack (Sinatra, Dean Martin, Sammy Davis Jr., Joey Bishop, and Peter Lawford) leading the way in the sixties, Vegas also became the Entertainment Capital of the World. Fabulous entertainment by Elvis, Judy Garland, Liberace, Wayne Newton, Barbra Streisand, Bette Midler, Celine Dion, Tom Jones, Nat King Cole, Danny Thomas, and an amazing array of other top performers even brought countless non-gamblers to Vegas over the years, though an estimated ninety percent of its thirty-six million annual visitors do manage to gamble a little (at least at the slots) while in the city.

The tradition of fabulous music, glamorous showgirls, comedy, and spectacular shows (by Cirque de Soleil and Siegfried & Roy, for example) has never let up.

The Moulin Rouge Hotel and Casino opened in May of 1955 as the first multi-racial or integrated hotel/casino in Vegas. The former heavyweight boxing champion Joe Louis was one of the owners, and the club there had incredible and very popular entertainment, including Davis, Ella Fitzgerald, Duke Ellington, Harry Belafonte, and the Tropi-Can-Can chorus line.

Performers from other Vegas clubs would come in after their own shows were over and jam with the Moulin Rouge's entertainers. Stars like Sinatra, Jack Benny, George Burns, Marlene Dietrich, and Nat King Cole were in its audiences, and the crowds followed them there. It became the hottest club in Vegas, and the casino raked the money in. The loss of so much business was too much for other major hotel/casinos/showrooms, apparently, because pressure was applied to all the right people. The Moulin Rouge lost its liquor license and, in October, the casino closed down. The hotel was open for just a few more years, and the building burned in 2003. For a while, though, the Moulin Rouge was ahead of its time and proved (along with the popularity of Davis as a valued member of the Rat Pack) that integration in Vegas could work.

In 1999, Vegas had over thirty-seven million tourists and was considered "the most visited city in the world." With the growth of hotels (including the Bellagio, Bally's, Mandalay Bay, Excalibur, Luxor, Treasure Island, Venetian, the Wynn Las Vegas, Mirage, and MGM Grand), Vegas houses hundreds of thousands of casino and hotel employees. It's the fastest growing city in America, with its population quadrupling from 1980 to 1999.

In the fifties, Vegas became the country's poker capital, and now it's the home of the World Series of Poker. Mechanical slot machines, which had been invented in 1895 by Charles Fey, began operating in the city—even finding homes in the airport and grocery stores—in 1931. Slot machines later became a $5 billion a year business for the city. At first, they were mainly used in casinos for women to wile away the time while the men played poker and other "hardcore" games of chance. Now, they're one of the most popular features for all the gamblers in Vegas' casinos.

The extremes of Vegas lend themselves well to the fantasy world of movies, so it's not surprising that the city has been the inspiration for or background of many movies through the years. Though the first to come to mind might be the Rat Pack's *Oceans Eleven* and the Elvis Presley-Ann Margret vehicle *Viva Las Vegas*, other films set here have included *The Godfather*, *Casino*, *Bugsy*, *Independence Day*, *Star Trek: The Experience*, *Honeymoon in Vegas*, *Indecent Proposal*, *The Misfits*, *Honey I Blew Up the Kid*, *Rush Hour 2*, *Robin and the Seven Hoods*, *Leaving Las Vegas*, and *Lady Luck*.

Vegas isn't just a glamorous city of entertainment and gambling, though. It also has had numerous heavyweight championship boxing matches, including Sonny Liston vs. Floyd Patterson, Muhammad Ali vs. Leon Spinks, and Evander Holyfield vs. Mike Tyson. The city has also had its share of tennis tournaments and NASCAR races. It also hosts the annual National Finals Rodeo of the Pro-Rodeo Cowboys' Association. Until recently it also boasted well-used golf courses, with the major hotels of the past advertising popular golf courses that were frequented by Dean Martin, Willie Nelson, Bob Hope, Bing Crosby, and other performers. Today's hotels have found other uses, such as expanded casino space and parking lots, for the land that once housed the golf courses.

2

VISIONS OF BENJAMIN "BUGSY" SIEGEL

B enjamin "Bugsy" Siegel carved his niche at the top of the historical Vegas totem pole when he envisioned the enormous possibilities of Vegas and helped create the initial luxury casino hotel in what is now the gambling Mecca of the world. Though the El Rancho Vegas and Frontier featured casinos, they were certainly not in the same class as his fabulous Flamingo. The Flamingo changed the then heavily western-cowboy themed Vegas hotel scene forever.

It's easy to see why Siegel has apparently chosen to take up permanent residence in his old, pardon the expression, haunt. Robert Allen of the Haunted Vegas Tours confides that "Bugsy's ghost has been seen thousands of times. At the Flamingo, they brag about Bugsy's ghost. If you go to our website, you'll see some of the pictures we've got. Some of the security guards will say, 'Yeah, I've seen some weird stuff here.'

"Bugsy's there. You can feel it if you're sensitive at all. You can definitely feel it, especially around the wedding chapel and

Benjamin "Bugsy" Siegel brought the mob to Vegas when he opened the Flamingo Hotel & Casino. *Public Domain—courtesy PDPhoto.org.*

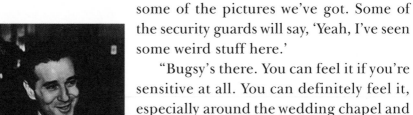

his monument, and they say he appears in the penthouse. See, the original hotel was torn down so Bugsy's quarters are gone, but they moved his pistachio green toilet and sink—it was all marble—up to one of the big suites. They say they've seen him up there. When you sleep, you can hear people playing pool, and you get up, and of course there's nothing going on but you can hear the balls being moved around."

A co-founder of Murder Inc., Siegel had the dubious honor of being the first to involve a crime syndicate in Vegas. He arrived in 1941, originally to begin a racewire service in the city where gambling was conveniently not outlawed. Siegel founded The Nevada Project Corporation of California, of which he was president and the largest stockholder, to officially provide the funding for the Flamingo. Meyer Lansky, Moe Sedway, and other major figures in the gangster world were the other shareholders.

Unfortunately for Siegel's lifespan, his fledgling Flamingo Hotel (named after his main girlfriend and rumored wife Virginia Hill's nickname or the flamingos near the Florida Hialeah racetrack, depending on whom you want to believe) failed to show sufficient initial profits to satisfy his mob partners. He would pay for supplies that were then stolen and resold to him later. The mob also believed Siegel was skimming money off the then astronomical more than $6 million construction funds (instead of the targeted $2 million) and gambling income. They thought he was sending it to secret Swiss bank accounts via Hill, whom he was said to have married secretly in Mexico, on her trips to Europe.

He refused to give the mob a full accounting of the money he'd spent on the hotel, then tried to obtain cash privately and, naturally, illegally.

Reportedly, Siegel also had confided in his longtime partner (and friend since they had been teenagers) Lansky that he planned to leave Vegas, taking his profits, to live in Europe in the near future. Siegel ignored Lansky's warning that the mob never would agree to his desertion of his responsibilities with them. He also refused "Lucky" Luciano's order to return control of the racewire to the mob in Chicago. As a result of all those factors, Siegel was said to have been the first gangster in Luciano's "Combination" to be sentenced to death by his fellow gangsters, including Luciano, Frank Costello, and a reluctant Lansky, when they met at the infamous Havana Conference in December 1946.

Lansky was able to persuade the others to give Siegel a little more time—during which the Flamingo began making a profit—but the hit still came down via four shots from a .30-calibre Army carbine rifle on June 20, 1947, while the forty-one-year-old Siegel was reading the *Los Angeles Times* and relaxing with his fellow gangster, Al Smiley, in Hill's Beverly Hills mansion. He had just returned from dinner at Jack's-at-the-Beach.

It was perfect timing since he was so paranoid that he rarely let his guard down. In fact, his palatial penthouse suite and office floor at the Flamingo sported bullet-proof windows and a secret exit

The memorial to Ben Siegel in the courtyard of the Flamingo, site of alleged hauntings. *Photo by Liz Cavanaugh.*

through a closet with a ladder leading into a tunnel, at the end of which a getaway limo and driver were waiting for him at all times. He also had the lock on his doors changed about once a week, waiting in the hall while the hotel's engineer, Don Garvin, changed them. Siegel's executor was never arrested, though he no doubt was rewarded quite well by the mob for his expert shots, which smashed Siegel's face, ribs, and neck vertebrae, tearing through his lungs and blowing his bright blue right eye onto the dining room floor, landing about fifteen feet from his body. It was a grisly ending for the psychopathic but movie-star handsome Siegel.

Only five relatives—no friends from the gangster world or Hollywood—came to his funeral. Ironically, both Lansky (in Havana) and Hill (on one of her jaunts to Zurich and its banks) were out of town and couldn't fly back in time.

In about twenty minutes after Siegel's death, Lansky's associates, Gus Greenbaum, Sedway, and Maurice Rosen, showed up at the Flamingo to take control for the Syndicate. Greenbaum took charge and operated the Flamingo at a great profit, with the mob controlling the hotel and casino until its purchase by Kirk Kerkorian in 1967.

One of his Hollywood friends, Frank Sinatra, did respect Siegel's memory enough to toast him at the site of his death just a few days afterward, according to Anthony Summers and Robbyn Swan in their book *Sinatra, The Life*.

Though Siegel was said to be charming and quite generous to charities and to his employees, who actually were fond of him, his hair-trigger temper still could cause him to become "buggy" when he was angry. Though it was an affectionate term of honor among other gangsters for one of their own who was completely fearless, Siegel really hated the nickname. Siegel earlier had to soothe his contracting foreman Del Webb, urging him to stop worrying about the possibility of being killed by gangsters, pragmatically stating, "There's no chance that you'd get killed. We only kill each other."

Siegel was born on February 28, 1906, in Brooklyn, New York. He and cinema's most famous gangster, George Raft, were

The wedding chapel of the Flamingo, complete with orb. *Photo by Liz Cavanaugh.*

close friends for many years. It's considered a toss up as to who influenced the other's dapper and elegantly suited style more as adults. Raft remained loyal to Siegel, even making a long, difficult trip in dangerous, rainy, and foggy weather driving from Hollywood (normally just a two-hour journey) to appear at the Flamingo's grand opening on December 26, 1946. Siegel had caused confusion by switching the date to December 28th, then back to the 26th. Despite the popular comedian, Jimmy Durante, as headliner, with Raft, Xavier Cugat's Orchestra, George Jessel, and Rose Marie (later of "The Dick Van Dyke Show" fame) being featured as the entertainers for the opening, it didn't turn out to be so grand. The weather conditions and an intimidating warning from newspaper mogul William Randolph Hearst led most of the invited celebrities to avoid the gala event, held on December 26, 1946, at the still-unfinished hotel. Rose Marie later recalled about thirty to forty stars, including Clark Gable, Joan Crawford, Caesar Romero, and Lana Turner, being guests at the opening, though the two Constellation planes

Siegel had chartered were unable to fly in the bad weather. Her memories of the opening differ, however, from those who have said considerably fewer (and mostly less prominent) stars were present at the dismal opening.

The hotel was still under construction, so guests had to stay at other hotels. The air-conditioning (the very first in Vegas) only worked sporadically, and the casino/hotel had to be shut down for a while just a month after the grand opening.

Siegel's own cherished ambitions for a Hollywood screen test were politely ignored by his movie pals, though he even studiously took acting lessons. After all, who would have been responsible for breaking the news to him if he didn't pass the audition?

Siegel probably would have been pleased that one of his daughters married comedian Jan Murray, bringing the show business world officially into his family.

Siegel and Lansky first met when they were fifteen years old and nineteen years old, respectively. They had teamed up in the early days in New York, guarding bootleggers trucks, operating the Bug and Meyer Mob (gangster protection and murder were their specialties), founding Murder Inc. (the first hit squad with contract killing of other mobsters), then eventually working together at the top of the criminal coalition called the Syndicate, which had a vast organization of bootlegging, illegal gambling, bookmaking, drugs, and prostitution. In the pre-instant news era of 1941, Siegel and Sedway took over the racewire operations in Vegas with Trans America Wire, making a fortune relaying thoroughbred horse race results to bookies nationwide. Though Nevada was the first state to make racewires legal, the pair not surprisingly weren't above using illegal methods—including murder—to gain control of the wires in Vegas. Siegel, in fact, is credited—or decried—as the first to invite the mob into Las Vegas.

William "Billy" Wilkerson, publisher of *The Hollywood Reporter* and owner of popular Hollywood nightclubs Ciro's and LaRue's, was the original developer of the resort hotel/casino which became the Flamingo, selling out to Siegel (except for a one-third interest) in the early stages. Siegel's vision was even grander than Wilkerson's had been, planning stables for forty horses, a nine-hole championship golf course, an upscale restaurant, a waterfall, gardens with beautiful landscaping (in a desert, remember), a health club, tennis courts, a huge swimming pool, 105 luxurious guest rooms with their own full baths (complete with bidet), a trapshooting range, a shopping area, facilities for badminton/squash/handball, palm trees, and, of course, a beautiful showroom featuring internationally famous performers. He even tried bringing in actual flamingos for the grounds, but the heat proved too much for the birds, so he gave that idea up fairly quickly.

Siegel was more than hands on, and his fingers allegedly were more than a little sticky. Siegel himself did invest quite a chunk of change, but most of the funds for the building and the necessary bribes to government officials, like—allegedly—Clark County Sheriff Glen Jones (who helped license the Flamingo and was forced to resign after soliciting bribes in the fifties) and Senator Pat McCarran (for whom the original airport was named), came from the Syndicate. The bribery worked after a stop work order had been given by the Civilian Public Administration because of short building supplies after the war, when returning veterans needed homes built. In a two-day hearing, somehow it was decided (after alleged perjury by the construction crew) that the crew was working on an earlier set of plans for the Flamingo, which had been approved before the freeze began, even though work wasn't underway until the second sets of plans had been drawn up (after the freeze had gone into effect).

J. Edgar Hoover and the FBI were determined to bring Siegel down, eventually compiling a file of 2,400 pages on the gangster, mainly by illegally bugging his phone lines and hotel suite. Their pressure on Siegel, with constant surveillance, didn't end in Siegel's imprisonment, but it may have contributed to his mob associates wanting him out of the way.

Lansky himself always denied mob involvement in Bugsy's murder. He tried to blame it on Hill's brother, saying he was angry because Siegel had mistreated Hill.

Since his death, Siegel has been lauded by many (and perhaps vilified by just as many) as the one person most responsible for turning the small Western town into the famous resort, gambling, and vacation Mecca it is today. The modern Flamingo Las Vegas, now owned by Harrah's Entertainment, is a four-towered Art Deco/Streamline Moderne styled neon pink hotel with 3,626 rooms on a forty-acre property. Siegel would be happy to know they finally found a way for a while to exhibit live flamingos in an outdoor habitat on site. Ah, the wonders of air-conditioning that actually worked. Now, the only flamingos there are neon, unless you count souvenirs featuring the pink long-legged birds.

The original hotel structure, which had been the film site for the "Rat Pack" original *Ocean's Eleven* in 1960 and for the Elvis/ Ann Margret movie *Viva Las Vegas,* was demolished on December 14, 1993, with the garden for the new hotel built on its site. The hotel was immortalized in the books *Fear and Loathing in*

The Beverly Hills mansion where Ben Siegel was murdered.
Public Domain—courtesy PDPhoto.org.

23

Las Vegas: A Savage Journey to the Heart of the American Dream by Hunter S. Thompson and *Last Call* by Tim Powers, as well as in cartoons (take-off versions of the hotel were featured in both *The Jetsons* and *Kim Possible*) and even a game (*Grand Theft Auto: San Andreas*). The Flamingo was mentioned in numerous other movies, novels, and television series. Of course, the 1991 movie *Bugsy*, featuring Warren Beatty, might be considered the ultimate "tribute" to Siegel and the Flamingo.

According to many eyewitnesses through the years since his murder, Siegel's spirit still remains in the desert city he considered his own. His debonair, smoking jacketed apparition has been spotted many times at the location of his Flamingo Presidential Suite (which still features his personally chosen pistachio green linoleum, toilets, and bidet), by the hotel's pool, the Presidential Suite, the wedding chapel, and the rose garden, which includes a monument in his honor. A shaken maid even quit her job at the hotel after exclaiming that she had seen Siegel's ghost on the fifth floor.

Intimidating enough in life (when you wouldn't dare call him "Bugsy" to his face), just imagine how startling it would be to see his close to six feet apparition in the moonlit garden of the Flamingo as you rounded a rosebush! Considering he personally admitted killing at least twenty people (some think at least thirty, supposedly killing his first when he was just sixteen years old) during his lifetime, it's not surprising Siegel would want to stick around in the updated version of his favorite luxury hotel instead of venturing on to his final "reward."

3

GANGSTERS—
THE REST OF THE STORY

Ben Siegel wasn't the only mobster in Vegas by a long shot. It was the ideal place for gangsters—legal casinos with private counting rooms where millions of dollars could be skimmed off the enormous profits. The mob (usually called "The Boys" in Vegas) settled in for about four decades of officially behind-the-scenes control of Vegas casinos, with their power there beginning to end around 1967 when Kirk Kerkorian bought the Flamingo and Howard Hughes bought the Desert Inn. When the Corporate Gaming Act was passed by the Nevada legislature, it changed everything by allowing public corporations to operate casinos. From that time, the Nevada Gaming Control Board required only the major operator in a corporation to have a background check.

Until that time, though, men like Moe Dalitz, Benny Binion, Frank Costello, Meyer and Jake Lansky, Gus Greenbaum (who, along with his wife, was brutally murdered when he quit running the Riviera for the mob and possibly had been caught skimming more than his share of profits), Mickey Cohen, Frank "Lefty" Rosenthal, Johnny Roselli (whose Friar's Club membership was sponsored by Frank Sinatra), Joey Adonis, Doc Stacher (the Sands), Anthony "Tony Batters" Accardo (the Sands), and Sam Giancana (the Desert Inn) were all actively, though often secretly, involved with investing in and operating both major and minor hotels and casinos in "Sin City." This included not just the Flamingo, but also the Thunderbird (opened by Lansky), Sands (opened by Longy Zwillman; headquarters for Frank Sinatra and his Summit, better known as the Rat Pack, who played the Copa Club there in legendary performances), Desert Inn (Dalitz), Dunes (New England mob), Stardust (taken over by The Chicago Outfit), Fremont, Aladdin, Caesars Palace, Hacienda, Tropicana (Costello and Carlos Marcello), Riviera (the Chicago Outfit), and even the family-oriented Circus Circus hotels and casinos.

The mobbed-up Jimmy Hoffa's Central States Pension Fund of the International Brotherhood of Teamsters provided generous loans for many Vegas casinos and hotels (including those for Caesars Palace and Circus Circus, among others), as did the Syndicate and other gangster groups and individuals. Hoffa was not himself a member of the mob, but he did provide those loans to them. It was after he had served time in prison for those connections to organized crime and subsequently discontinued his relationship with the mob that Hoffa disappeared without a trace.

Meyer Lansky was one of the first, along with his pal Siegel, to realize the potential of the Nevada city. He was largely responsible for the Mob's allowing his old friend Siegel to take control of Vegas. He also convinced the federal government to release Mafia boss Lucky Luciano from prison after Lansky helped provide security from German submarines for military ships being built in the New York harbor. Luciano, who basically was the founder of the American

Mafia, was released and then deported to Italy as a result. Lansky was a part of the WWII Operation Underworld of the Office of Naval Intelligence and also had helped break up Nazi rallies in New York prior to the war. "The Boys" may have been ruthless criminals, but at least they were patriotic.

Lucky Luciano, who controlled much of Vegas' mob activities from exile in Cuba and Italy. *Public Domain—courtesy PDPhoto.org.*

Lansky had pleaded with his fellow gangsters not to kill Siegel during two meetings in Cuba, though he ultimately wasn't successful after the third meeting. Lansky continued his involvement with the Flamingo for the next two decades following Siegel's death. He also is said to have been instrumental in helping Accardo of the Chicago Outfit take control of Vegas away from the New York mob.

Dalitz was beloved in the city, even called "Mr. Las Vegas" because of his frequent charitable contributions. The fact that he had been a bootlegger during Prohibition and had run the Mayfield Road Gang in Cleveland prior to his move to Vegas was basically ignored. Robert Kennedy wasn't fooled. In his book, *The Enemy Within*, he claimed Dalitz was a "Las Vegas and Havana gambling figure." The FBI, though, was repeatedly frustrated by their inability to find enough evidence against Dalitz that could have been presented successfully in court.

During his forty years in Vegas, Dalitz contributed enormously to the development of casinos on the Strip (which had been named by former Los Angeles vice squad commander Guy McAfee when he opened the 91 Club on old Highway 91). Dalitz was the real opener and operator of the Desert Inn (fronted by Wilbur Clark) and also secretly ran the Riviera. He also successfully brought suit against *Penthouse* magazine for a story that had stated he was connected to organized crime. He sold the Desert Inn to Howard Hughes in 1967 for $14.6 million.

Binion deserves the gratitude of millions of thirsty tourists. He supposedly was the first to give free drinks to gamblers when he opened Binion's Horseshoe Casino, saying he wanted to "make little people feel like big people."

Jack Entratter ran the entertainment and showroom at the Sands hotel, where the Rat Pack performed, for Lansky. The Sands gave free rooms and drinks to its gamblers. Entratter and casino boss Carl Cohen later sold it to Hughes in the billionaire's purchase of six mobbed-up hotels.

The Dunes, built with money from the Teamsters Pension Fund and the mob, was owned by Morris Shenker, who was

3. Gangsters—The Rest of the Story

associated with Lansky, Hoffa, and the St. Louis Mafia. Shenker himself was investigated by St. Louis's Organized Crime Strike Force.

When the mob lost its holdings in Cuba after Castro's takeover, Vegas was the natural new home for the gambling and other activities that had formerly created such a bonanza of business (millions of dollars each year) for the mob.

The FBI tried for years to get evidence about mobsters skimming gambling profits in the counting rooms, but they had illegally wiretapped the casinos (at the Sands, Desert Inn, Stardust, and others) so none of the evidence they had so painstakingly obtained was admissible in court. FBI reports say that the skim from major Vegas casinos during the late fifties averaged roughly a million dollars a day. Because it wasn't officially counted, no taxes were paid on the skimmed amount. No wonder "The Boys" loved Vegas.

Many residents of Vegas felt—and still feel—that mob control in the casinos wasn't such a bad thing because those in charge usually did a good job of kicking out all the other criminals from the city. That sense of residential security ended when Anthony "Tony the Ant" Spilotro (who had been an enforcer in Chicago and Vegas before becoming the top mobster in Vegas) didn't go along with the long-time mob quasi-gentlemanly attitude of aiming violence in Vegas only against other gangsters. He and his brother Michael ended up beaten by baseball bats and buried alive in Indiana after a series of high-profile crimes by the brothers' violent "Hole in the Wall Gang."

"Tony the Ant" Spilotro had first opened a gift shop in the Circus Circus Casino under the name Anthony Stuart. Later, five of the casino's employees were found buried outside Vegas in the desert. Spilotro was indicted but acquitted in the Foreman murder case in Chicago in 1972. Then he went back to skimming casino money, was indicted again, and once again acquitted when the star witness was murdered. He and Frank Rosenthal of the Stardust Casino worked together, but Spilotro couldn't enter any casinos after he was put on the infamous Vegas Black Book in 1979. That's when he and the "Hole in the Wall Gang" began their jewel heists.

This was one of the factors that is said to have helped end the mob era in the city, as did federal prosecutions and convictions in the eighties and the 1993 imprisonment of the last head of the mob in Vegas, Don "The Wizard of the Odds" Angelina. Many were imprisoned because of testimony by Frank Cullotta, who had worked closely with Spilotro and who had to enter the witness protection program afterward. This was said to be a main cause of The Chicago Outfit (the Chicago Family of La Casa Nostra) losing control in Sin City.

Visitors to Vegas are still fascinated by its mob history. Guests can check into The Gangster Room and even have a gangster themed wedding at the Ron Decar's Las Vegas Hotel. Retired FBI agent Ellen Knowlton and her not-for-profit museum organization are planning to open a Gangster Museum in Vegas by 2010, in a three-story brick federal building which was built in 1933. The museum is being designed by Dennis Barrie, who also designed the Rock and Roll Hall of Fame in Cleveland. Plans call for it to include historical documents, like photographs and wiretap transcripts about Vegas' organized crime and all the work that law enforcement, including the FBI, undertook to end the mob's power there.

4

HOWARD HUGHES

When Howard Hughes first started visiting Las Vegas, it was as a dashing, handsome young aviator and wealthy-beyond-belief playboy movie producer/director who always seemed to date the most gorgeous Hollywood stars (Jean Harlow, Katharine Hepburn, Rita Hayworth, Lana Turner, Yvonne De Carlo, Ava Gardner, Olivia de Havilland, and Ginger Rogers among them). Reporters and photographers upset De Carlo when they hung around the couple after he took her out to dinner at the Flamingo Hotel. He had them effectively bribed with bottles of expensive whiskey, and Hughes and De Carlo had privacy the rest of their Vegas trip.

On another trip to Vegas—this time in 1944—Hughes was watching Liberace rehearse at the Last Frontier Hotel. Liberace mistook him for a lighting engineer, instructing him to turn up the blue light when he began playing "Claire de Lune." It's easy to imagine the performer's embarrassment when the entertainment director walked over and introduced him to the famous movie maker/aviator.

Hughes tended to escape to Vegas every now and then through the decades, when things in Los Angeles overwhelmed him. He was a night owl, partly because he was often in such pain that he couldn't sleep, so Vegas was his kind of town, especially when he still wanted to enjoy the shows—and the showgirls.

He had discovered Harlow for his film *Hell's Angels*, which boasted the most expensive production ($3.8 million) of any movie of its time. It featured what are to this day still considered some of the most incredible aircraft scenes, some of which were air stunts by Hughes himself, in movie history.

Hughes, who was owner of RKO Studios, counted actors like Cary Grant and Randolph Scott as his friends for decades. For their films, Hughes even designed special lingerie, which he considered engineering challenges, for Harlow and Jane Russell (most famously her quite uplifting half-cup bra). In one of her starring roles, Russell was in the movie *The Las Vegas Story* for Hughes' studio. Two of his other controversial hit movies were *Scarface* and *The Outlaw*. In 1954, Hughes became the only individual in movie history to be sole owner of a film studio, when he bought out the other stockholders.

Howard had inherited (and subsequently fought hard to retain) control of the Hughes Tool Company when he was just eighteen years old. He bought out his relatives' shares of stock so he would be the sole stockholder in the company. His father, Howard Robard Hughes Sr., had built the company and his fortune on a drill bit he invented—the first drill bit capable of penetrating solid rock to get to the oil underneath. His son later became an inventor himself.

When he was just eleven, he set up Houston's first wireless broadcast system. At twelve, he built the first motorized bicycle in Houston from parts of his father's steam engine. At the age of fourteen, Howard began taking flying lessons and also convinced his father to purchase an expensive new Stutz Bearcat for the sole purpose of his taking it apart and putting it back together. He accomplished this task which he'd set for himself in less than a month. The younger Hughes was considered widely to be a genius involving science, automotive, and air flight matters. As an adult, Hughes built Trans World Airlines into a powerful international airline. He became an aviation hero on a par with Charles Lindbergh, setting several world flight records. He was known as a ruthless businessman, a generous though completely unfaithful lover, and an adventurer who was most alive flying his beloved planes. He also became the richest man in America.

Hughes was an honored pilot, winning the 1934 All-America Air Meet, setting a new speed record in 1935, and setting two new transcontinental flight records. He built and test-piloted the H-1 airplane and piloted a Lockheed 14 on an around-the-world flight that beat Lindbergh's New York to Paris record, cutting the time in half. He even was awarded a special Congressional Gold Medal.

Hughes was the first to create a nonstop coast-to-coast passenger air service (ten hour flights, with comfortable seating) in America. He invented power steering, better cockpits, and an advanced hydraulic system, all put to good use in his TWA flights. His Constellation planes were fast and dependable, with regular flight schedules. He designed and built a large "flying boat" that no one else thought could fly. It was laughingly called the Spruce Goose, but Hughes proved it could fly by piloting it himself in 1947. In the next decade, he again was a pioneer, manufacturing spy satellites for the government. His Hughes Aircraft Company, a division of Hughes Tool Company, came up with many advancements in aeronautical technology and became the third largest supplier of military weapons control/delivery systems in America.

His talents and brilliance are two of the reasons it's so sad that younger generations doubtless will best remember Hughes as the gaunt and paranoid recluse with a stringy beard and unwashed long hair. He was so terrified of germs from other people that he paradoxically refused to allow his suite at Vegas' Desert Inn hotel to be cleaned by hotel staff during his four years in residence. His inches-long fingernails and toenails grew to grotesque lengths because he didn't want anyone to touch him. If he (or those working for him) had to touch things like door handles, it was done with layers upon layers of tissues (his best friend at that point) shielding hands from any germs that might be lurking.

One amusing story tells why visitors to the Desert Inn over a certain year period had Hughes to thank for an ice cream treat. In what was one of his obsessions over a certain food, Hughes wanted plenty of Baskin-Robbins banana nut ice cream on hand while he was living in the hotel. The company had quit making the formula, so Hughes had a special order for a minimum run of 350 gallons made up just for him. Within days of the arrival of his much-desired ice cream, Hughes decided he only wanted French vanilla ice cream from that point. So the Desert Inn casino's guests were gifted with pints of free banana nut ice cream until the order ran out.

That wasn't his only dining peculiarity, either. He only ate peas with a special fork that allowed peas he thought were too large to fall through the tines. He checked his squares of chocolate cake with a ruler to make sure the Desert Inn's chef had cut it exactly right. He would become obsessed with a particular food (roast beef sandwiches or Swanson's turkey frozen television dinners, for example), then suddenly tire of them and never eat them again.

A complicated set of physical and mental conditions worked together to deteriorate the health of Hughes' brilliant mind and rangy body. He had an extreme case of obsessive-compulsive disorder (not understood at the time), over a dozen head injuries (and subsequent brain damage only determined positively from his autopsy results) from various accidents and crashes, excruciating migraines, almost lifelong deafness, and addiction to pain-killing drugs (such as intravenous codeine) for severe pain from back injuries suffered in aircraft crashes, as well as tertiary syphilis. Among the symptoms of the last condition are paranoia, confusion, and deterioration of the patient's thought processes, all of which were famously suffered by Hughes.

The deafness was caused by a genetic disease called otosclerosis, which caused almost constant whistling and ringing in his ears (except when plane or car engines drowned out the sound), and sleeplessness (staying awake for days at a time on occasion). For many years, he steadfastly refused to wear hearing aids and had to try to read lips or remain isolated from others. No wonder he relied so much on lengthy memos for communication much of his life.

Hughes also had survived a diagnosed case of spinal meningitis. Some of the symptoms of undiagnosed illnesses during his lifetime were possibly psychosomatic, though, caused by the long-time hypochondria which had been exacerbated in childhood by the desire to capture his parents' attention and sympathy. Both parents had passed away when he was a socially insecure teenager: his mother at thirty-nine and his father at fifty-four, when Howard was sixteen and eighteen, respectively. His mother, Allene Gano Hughes, also had obsessive-compulsive disorder and had drilled into her son an overwhelming fear of germs and the chance of contamination from others that just became more intense in his mind and behavior as the years went by.

On Thanksgiving Day, November 27, 1966, Hughes was carried on a stretcher to the ninth-floor penthouse at the Desert Inn. The business operations for his two billion dollars empire would be overseen from two large suites on the eighth floor. His reservation was for just ten days, but he stayed for four years, finally leaving when his concerns about atomic testing in the area were disregarded. After that ten-day period in 1966, though, he refused to be forced from the hotel by owners Moe Dalitz and Ruby Kolod, who had booked the suite out to the casino's best customers for the popular tourist Christmas season. Though Hughes had been a huge (and very unlucky) gambler in this past, he no longer hit the casinos, nor did his Mormon employees. So it's no wonder they wanted to kick Hughes and his entourage out of the hotel so the high-rollers could have their suites. Hughes told his reliable right-hand man Robert Maheu (who never, in the fourteen years he worked for him, actually saw his boss in person) to handle it. Maheu, a veteran of both the CIA and the FBI, ran Summa Corporation, the holding company for his Nevada businesses. After a chain of intervention from Maheu, mobster Johnny Rosselli, and Teamster boss Jimmy Hoffa with owners Dalitz and Kolod, Hughes bought the Desert Inn hotel and casino for a mere $13.25 million in April of 1967. That's one way to extend your reservation.

Hughes decided he liked buying up Las Vegas properties (which many believe to have been his plan all along), adding to his acquisitions the Frontier ($23 million), the Sands ($23 million), the Castaways ($3.3 million), the Silver Slipper ($5.4 million), the Landmark ($17.3 million), KLAS-TV ($3.6 million), the North Las Vegas Airport, and the land now occupied by Treasure Island, the Mirage, and the Fashion Show Mall. As Steve Fischer points out in his entertaining and informative book *When the Mob Ran Vegas: Stories of Money, Mayhem and Murder*, the two things that the hotels he bought had in common were that Meyer Lansky was involved with each of them and they all had outstanding loans with Jimmy Hoffa's Central States Teamsters Pension Fund. Hughes' hotel/casino buying spree of about $300 million only came to a halt when Nevada refused to allow his purchase of the Stardust Hotel because of government worries that he was gaining a monopoly. Before he was red-lighted, though, he had taken over twenty percent of the hotels on the Vegas Strip alone.

He didn't stop at just hotels and casinos, though. He bought almost all the silver and gold mines in Nevada while he was in a spending mood. He also became the owner of Vera Krupp's Spring Mountain Ranch, which he bought in an unsuccessful effort to lure his wife Jean Peters away from California and keep his marriage (such it was) intact. She finally divorced him because he was incapable of more than a telephone relationship at that point in his life.

Hughes became the largest landowner in the state during this period, in fact. It wasn't just like a real-life Monopoly game to him, though. The purchases all gave him a great tax break, too, which was a significant factor since the TWA sale in May that year had boosted his income by about $546 million—half a billion dollars. The tax rate was a lot higher on unused income than on active income. The Nevada buying spree certainly counted as active income.

He bought the KLAS television station because he wanted to control the viewing hours and the late night movies the station played. At that point in his life, he was still up until all hours, but he no longer went out on the town. His only entertainment was making deals, writing voluminous memos on yellow legal pads, and watching his favorite movies all night.

There are two versions of the actual reason he decided to buy the Silver Slipper. The first (and most widely circulated) is that the famous lighted slipper sign was across from his bedroom suite, and he found its movements to be irritating. Since he had blackout curtains on the bedroom window, though, the second version may be more accurate. The next story is that, being highly paranoid, he believed he was being spied on by a photographer secreted in the hollow center of the turning slipper sign. Either way, he bought the Silver Slipper, filled in the slipper sign's center with concrete and kept that "damn slipper from rotating." And it only cost him $5.4 million to take care of that little problem.

Hughes actually did have plans to change things in Vegas, wanting to end the mob's control and improve the city's image. He was the first individual to own a resort casino, and he legitimized Vegas in many people's eyes.

Poker champion and singer/songwriter Sunset Slim recalls a rare encounter with the reclusive billionaire. "I saw Howard Hughes in Vegas once. It was during the two days he disappeared from the Desert Inn. He was downtown near the Golden Nugget and Horseshoe, wearing forties-style pleated pants and a hound's-tooth jacket with patches, holding an expensive little Oriental pearl pipe, with his long hair and his long beard. I had to say something to him, so I asked how he was doing. He mumbled he was okay and how about me. Then he realized somebody might have recognized him and took off."

Hughes had pulled disappearing acts for years. In 1932, he left Los Angeles with no one else's prior knowledge and used an alias so he would be hired by American Airlines as a baggage handler and pilot-in-training. His abilities were so superb that he worked his way up to co-pilot within just a few weeks, only abandoning the job when someone finally recognized him. Friends said he always was happiest in the sky, so he may have regretted having to go back to his more famous identity and lifestyle.

While he lived in Vegas, he become more and more dependent on drugs to control his constant pain. He would intermittently be coherent, and then would sink back into a stupor. Because of his phobias, he always was alone, nude, and unwashed, afraid to touch anything or come in contact with anyone. The blackout curtains on his sealed rooms shut him away from the world even further, with the flickering light from his television his only company. He had all the power anyone could want, but wasn't able to enjoy it.

When a power coup by Bill Gray, the leader of what was unofficially termed the Mormon Mafia, took control of Hughes from Maheu, Hughes and his entourage suddenly left Vegas in 1970, without a word to Maheu or anyone else. They traveled under the radar to the Bahamas. Hughes intended to return later to Vegas, but Gray and his group wouldn't allow that. They wanted to keep him out of the country and under their control. When Hughes told one of his aides that he wanted to stop living in dark hotel rooms, buy a yacht, and cruise the Mediterranean, the aide was fired by Gray. Then Hughes was told that Maheu wanted to kidnap him. He was then put back to bed, and his drug doses were increased by forty times their previous dosage, according to Peter Harry Brown and Pat H. Broeske in their fine biography, *Howard Hughes: The Untold Story*.

Brown and Broeske also described his next unsuccessful bids for independence. He walked into a hotel in Vancouver instead of using his wheelchair and said he didn't want blackout coverings on the picture window overlooking the ocean. He was hustled back into bed and drugged after being warned helicopters could fly by the window after taking surreptitious photos of him. The one that almost worked was when he went to London, contacted his old flying companion Jack Real, detoxed himself, and began flying again. He happily piloted four long flights before he fell in his hotel suite, underwent hip surgery, and became re-addicted to pain medications. That was the end of his brief time back in the world. Gray and company allegedly made sure of that. He never did make it back to Vegas, as he had planned. His old friend Cary Grant sadly told London's *Times* that Hughes' soul and mind were dead after that.

In 1976, Hughes' frail body finally gave out at the age of seventy on a plane en route from Mexico to his hometown of Houston, Texas. His body was so unrecognizably emaciated (just ninety pounds on his six-foot-four body) that it had to be identified through his fingerprints. Courts ruled that he died without a valid will, and the battle over his estate was won by twenty-two cousins from both sides of his family. Disputes over inheritance tax were reviewed three times by America's Supreme Court.

His Howard Hughes Medical Institute, which he had begun planning when he was just twenty-five years old, has become America's biggest private sponsor of biomedical research. He funded the institute by handing it all the stock of the billion dollars a year Hughes Aircraft Company, which caused it to be a tax-exempt charity. Yes, it was another big tax break. Hughes wasn't exactly a generous philanthropist, but nobody ever said he was stupid.

Doctors for his estate claimed later that Hughes' death was caused largely by the neglect of his Mormon so-called caretakers, who allegedly schemed to gain control of his money by keeping him sedated and pliable (so he would sign their papers or just plain not pay attention to everything they were doing behind his back) by means of Valium, Seconal, Librium, and injectable codeine. A billion dollars worth of government securities, savings certificates, and cash vanished from his accounts, while his aides received enormous pay raises and benefit packages and supposed verbal approval for huge purchases that he never gave written authorization for, unlike the days so soon before when he wrote his customary extensive memos and highly detailed instructions to his staff.

For years in his earlier life, when he survived aerial crashes, it had seemed likely that Hughes would die in one of his planes. Ironically, that's just what happened, though the famous aviator wasn't the one in control of his last flight.

5

CAROLE LOMBARD DEATH MYSTERIOUS AND FASCINATING

Carole Lombard sits at number twenty-three of fifty of the American female screen legends, according to the American Film Institute's assessment in 1999. She has had numerous honors, including a star on the Hollywood Walk of Fame and a nomination for an Academy Award for Best Actress for her work in the film *My Man Godfrey*.

Lombard has one other distinction which family and friends would rather forget. She was the first female casualty in World War II. The singer was killed when the plane in which she was a passenger crashed into a mountain about twenty miles outside of Las Vegas on January 16, 1942. Lombard was returning to Los Angeles after attending a war bond rally in Indiana. She was very patriotic and had raised more than two million dollars' worth of war bonds during the visit.

The TWA flight took off on the morning of January 16th, making several stops along the way for refueling. The last stop, in Las Vegas, was a variation of the schedule, which many say was the reason the plane crashed into Mount Potosi instead of flying high enough to go over its 8,500 peak. The takeoff occurred after dark, but reports say the weather was clear in the city when the pilot headed west for Los Angeles.

As with any crash in wartime, suspicions were raised about possible sabotage. There were also other allegations of sightings of lights in the sky prior to the plane's takeoff and warnings from Lombard's mother that it wasn't safe to fly that day. When all the information comes together, it makes for an interesting yet sad story.

Lombard was born October 6, 1908, in Fort Wayne, Indiana and named Jane Alice Peters. She was the youngest of three children born to Frederick C. and Elizabeth Peters. After her parents divorced, Carole's mother took her and her two brothers to Los Angeles in 1914. Carole was discovered by film director Allan Dwan when he saw her playing baseball. She was only twelve, but he had a role for her—that of a tomboy in the movie *A Perfect Crime*. She did several low-budget films before being signed to Fox Film Corporation in 1925. Her first sound film was *High Voltage* in 1929. In 1930, she moved over to Paramount Pictures, where she had several supporting actress roles. Finally, she was cast as a lead opposite John Barrymore in *Twentieth Century*, where director Howard Hawks allowed her real personality to be filmed. Critics and fans saw a new Lombard, and she soon found herself in major films including *Bolero* with George Raft and *Hands Across the Table*, which helped her to become known as a comedy actress.

She followed with the popular *My Man Godfrey* and *Nothing Sacred*. She had hoped to star as Scarlett O'Hara alongside her new husband, Clark Gable, in *Gone With The Wind*, but that was not to be. She found herself starring with James Stewart in *Made For Each Other* and with Cary Grant in *In Name Only*, as well as working with Alfred Hitchcock in *Mr. & Mrs. Smith*. She was then cast in what was to be her last film, *To Be Or Not To Be*, co-starring with Jack Benny.

Lombard was not immune to her leading men. After meeting William Powell in 1930 while working on *Man of the World* and *Ladies Man*, they married the next year, only to divorce two years later. The two stayed friends and worked on other movies together. She had several other liaisons, including actors Gary Cooper and George Raft, plus screenwriter Robert Riskin. She also dated singer Russ Columbo and was said to have been very serious about him. The singer was killed in a gun accident, and Lombard was devastated. Known as an extravagant hostess with elaborate parties, Carole is said to have had one more huge party after Columbo's death. Following that, reports are that she stopped giving the parties where she invited everyone she knew and turned instead to small private gatherings.

Lombard met Clark Gable in 1932, when they co-starred in *No Man Of Her Own*. In 1936, the two became involved, even while the actor was married to Ria Langham. After a fan magazine outed the couple, the studio gave Gable an ultimatum: marry Lombard or leave her alone. Gable divorced Langham, and he and Carole were married on March 29, 1939. They lived on a ranch in Encino, California, and most of the people who knew them acknowledged that he considered her the love of his life, even though it was widely known that he continued to have extra-marital affairs after their marriage.

Lombard was very patriotic, and she readily agreed when she was asked to do the war bond rally in Indianapolis, Indiana, the month after the Japanese attacked Pearl Harbor. She traveled to the rally with her mother and press agent, who went with her because Gable was unable to do so. She raised more than two million dollars, triple the amount the government anticipated would be raised. The trio finished the rally and went immediately to the airport, where they arrived around 4am. The press agent, Otto Winkler, wanted to take time to get some rest, or take a train where they could sleep. Lombard wanted to board the plane and head home.

Here is where things start to get interesting. According to published reports, there were many situations and circumstances that followed her decision that made her death somewhat mysterious and intriguing. One of the reasons given as to why she decided to fly home is that Gable was starting to film a movie with Lana Turner, and Lombard wanted to be there and on the set when filming started. Carole insisted on the flight, despite the fact that her mother told her they should not fly. Apparently, Parker was a numerologist, and she told Carole that flying on January 16 was not a good thing to do. She also pointed out that the number three, which is a sign of bad luck, continued to appear in different aspects of the trip. Carole was thirty-three; there were three people traveling together, and the airline route designation was number three. Mother and daughter argued, and the press agent decided to flip a coin to see which way they should travel. Carole won the toss, and they boarded the airliner.

Weird things continued to happen on the flight. When they stopped in St. Louis, Missouri, at Lambert Field, the flight was delayed for two hours because some kind of smoke appeared that cut visibility to two miles. Interestingly, before the flight landed, the sky was clear and visibility was at twelve miles.

In Albuquerque, New Mexico, where the plane made a second stop, airline officials tried to get Lombard to take another flight so that some military pilots, who actually had the rank to take her seat, could fly on to their destination. It is said that she used her wit and charm to influence the officials to allow her party to remain on the flight.

After leaving New Mexico, the flight should have gone straight on to the Burbank Airport just south of Los Angeles. What was termed unusual headwinds caused the plane to use more fuel than usual, so it was scheduled to stop in Boulder City, Colorado, to refuel. At this point, the flight was some three hours late, and they couldn't make Boulder by dark. Boulder didn't have runway lights because the war department had ordered airports to cut their lights off after dark. The flight was routed to Las Vegas Army Airfield, now Nellis Air Force Base in Las Vegas, which had just been allowed to light one of its strips at night so flights could land and take off from that field.

The plane took off from Las Vegas at 7:07pm in a very clear sky. It is said that pilot bulletins warned flights to climb to an altitude of 10,000 feet to fly over the 8,500 foot-high Mount Potosi. At 7:20pm, the airplane hit the mountain at full speed. Speculation is that the pilot of the plane, Wayne C. Williams, had set his course for 8,000 feet when it was thought he would leave out of Boulder and he never reset that calculation. Pilot error was given as the cause of the accident, although several other things were investigated before that was declared.

FBI files were declassified in 1985 and revealed some very interesting information. A rancher reported seeing a mysterious light in the sky just above the peak of Mount Potosi moments before the plane went down. He said the light was there during the crash, then he didn't see it afterwards. Also in the report was a notarized report from a mechanic for the Civil Aeronautics Board who saw a similar light a few days before the crash, in the same spot. He states that he was sure it was not a star because it was much brighter and it was only there a short amount of time.

One of the investigations regarding the flight was that it might have been an act of sabotage. One of the people who gave up their seat in Albuquerque was violinist Joseph Szigeti. The Hungarian violinist was later cleared of any wrongdoing when it was determined that pilot error caused the crash.

Around 7:07, Williams reported that he was a little off course, about thirty-five miles west of Las Vegas. That was about the same time miners in the mountains heard an explosion and observed the fiery crash. They say flames shot up from the top of the mountain, and then faded. O.E. Salyer, a purchasing agent for the Blue Diamond Mine, reported the crash to TWA headquarters at Las Vegas. Dan Yanish, a watchman at the mine, observed the plane as it flew over the mine. He said the night was clear enough for a person to see for miles. He reported that just as the airplane was slipping into the distance he saw a flash and then flames rising from the mountain. Lee Houston, who was employed by the Blue Diamond Mine, had enough presence of mind to drive stakes in the ground to track the direction of the flames from the mine. Searchers used this information to determine where to start the climb and search for the downed aircraft.

Several hours after the miners saw the crash, Art Cheney, a pilot for Western Airlines, who was on a flight from Los Angeles to Las Vegas, saw the airliner in flames. When the investigation was finally over, it was determined that the pilot, who had already been called out for not following the flight instructions he had been given, had decided to take a shortcut through a restricted area to make up for lost time. He was about six miles off the original course. Unfortunately, the plane's flight records were lost in the crash so there was no data to explain why he took a different route or what really caused the accident. Searchers could find no trace of the pilot's flight plan or navigation log which would have indicated the course he was following when the plane hit the mountain. It is thought that because he was off-course, the 8,000-foot altitude that was on his original plan was not enough to get him over the peak, which was 8,500 feet where he crashed. During the hearings, there was also speculation that the cockpit lights were on, making it difficult for the two men piloting the plane to see the mountain looming in front of them even though it was a clear night.

A search party under the direction of Major W.H. Anderson, executive officer of the Air Corps gunnery school at nearby McCarren Field, set out on horseback, led by Indian tracker Tweed Wilson. The party found its way through the steep trails of the mountain, which was covered in snow at that time of the year. Ambulances and a group of rescue workers waited at the bottom of the mountain in case there were survivors. From the outset, most of the party figured that there would be no survivors. They could not even begin the search until the next morning because of the dangerous territory they had to cover in order to get to where the plane went down. It took them fourteen hours to reach the wreckage and confirm that everyone on the airplane was dead.

In Los Angeles, Gable and representatives from the studio, as well as Lombard's brothers, prepared to fly to Las Vegas. Although he wanted to join the search party when he arrived, friends persuaded Gable not to do so. Gable retired to Goodsprings, Nevada, located near the base of the mountain, to set up base. It is said he had a room at the Goodsprings Hotel but spent much of his time at the Pioneer Saloon awaiting word from searchers. Owners of the Pioneer Saloon claim you can still see the burn holes where Gable let his cigarettes slip from his fingers while he awaited news of his wife. They also say that a melted piece of aluminum that rests on top of their old pot-bellied stove was recovered from the site of the crash.

The search party found their worst nightmare when they reached the crash site. The twenty-two bodies were burned and mangled from being thrown from the plane, which hit the mountain and slid into a ravine. Pine trees in the plane's flight patch were burned and torn and there was no snow from the point where the airplane caught on fire.

The very determined fan, historian, or curiosity seeker can still climb to the site of the crash, even though the road to the top of Mt. Potosi is closed to the public. It requires a good deal of hiking and use of a four-wheel drive to get to the area. When the site is found, there is still a great deal of debris from the wreckage. Protocol requires that nothing be removed from the site although that surely has been defied as more and more people discover how to get there. One party that braved the climb reported that they found not only remnants from the airplane, but plastic bottles, paper, and other objects obviously left there by people who had been before them.

Other interesting facts about Lombard and Gable:

✳ Lombard was declared the first women killed in the line of duty during World War II, and Franklin Delano Roosevelt posthumously awarded her the Presidential Medal of Freedom.

✳ Gable attended the launch of the Liberty ship *SS Lombard* on January 15, 1944.

✳ The producer's of *To Be Or Not To Be* cut one of Lombard's lines in the film. The line? Carole's character asked, "What can happen in a plane?"

✳ On January 18, 1942, Jack Benny, who co-starred with Lombard in *To Be Or Not To Be*, didn't do his normal show out of respect for the actress. His show that night was all music.

✳ Lombard had signed on to do the film *They All Kissed The Bride* before her death. Joan Crawford was cast in that role. Crawford donated the money she made from the film to the Red Cross because she said she knew the only way she got the role was because of Lombard's death.

✳ Lombard's wedding ring was never found. Supposedly, Gable sent out search parties every year in the hopes of finding the ring and Carole's *V for Victory* brooch.

✳ One of Lombard's heart-shaped clips was found among the wreckage. It is said that Gable had it made into a locket and wore it every day.

✳ Lombard and Clark Gable are buried side by side at Forest Lawn Memorial Park Cemetery in Glendale, California. Her mother, Elizabeth Peters, is buried beside them.

✹ There is a memorial of sorts in Las Vegas to Lombard. Visitors to the Lowden Veterans Center and Museum can see a display of things recovered at the crash site, including hair barrettes, belt buckles, garter belt fasteners, molten pieces of aluminum, a pilot's control column from the DC-3, and spark plugs. There is also a January 17, 1942, edition of the *Boston Evening Globe* with the newspaper article about the crash.

✹ People who follow the history of the movies of the time believe Lombard would have been a huge star had she lived. Her final film, *To Be Or Not To Be*, was considered by critics to be her best performance. Because she would probably have continued to use her celebrity to do other war bond rallies and promote patriotism throughout the war, she would have been poised to take the big screen by storm when the war ended.

✹ After Lombard's death, Gable joined the U.S. Army Air Force. He received a special assignment in aerial gunnery, went through USAAF OCS Class 42-E training in Miami Beach, Florida, and was commissioned as a second lieutenant. He ranked 700th in a class of 2,600. Gable was the keynote speaker at the class's graduation. The actor was then assigned to make a recruiting film in order to recruit gunners. He went to England to make the film. He achieved the rank of captain while he was with the 351st at Pueblo Army Air Base in Colorado. He spent most of the war in the United Kingdom with the 351st, flying five combat missions and earning the Air Medal and the Distinguished Flying Cross. Before he was discharged in 1944, he achieved the rank of major.

✹ Lucille Ball, who was a good friend of Lombard's, says in her autobiography that she made the decision to leave film for television and the *I Love Lucy* series because of her friend. Ball swears that Carole came to her in a dream and told her to take a chance on the at-the-time unknown and somewhat risky realm of television. One account says she tried to tell Gable about the incident, but he apparently didn't believe that someone might speak to a person after his or her death.

6

THE BARONESS

Before Richard Burton bought the 33.6 karat Krupp diamond for then-wife Elizabeth Taylor in 1968 for $305 thousand at a Sotheby's auction, it was the prize possession of Vera Krupp. Vera was famously married to Baron Alfried Krupp, the German munitions millionaire who supplied the Nazi Army with weapons in World War II. A former actress in the German theatre, the naturalized American citizen left Baron Krupp in 1956, after three years of not-so-happily wedded bliss, to live at the Spring Mountain Ranch, about fifteen miles west of Vegas in a stunningly beautiful canyon. She bought the 520-acre ranch in Red Rock Canyon from Chet Lauck, a star of the popular Lum & Abner radio show, after she divorced Krupp in Vegas.

Like Ben "Bugsy" Siegel, the Baroness had a fondness for secret passages, with a closet leading to a corridor hiding a concealed bathroom and bedroom. Too bad she couldn't escape to that passage on April 10, 1959 when three thieves blindfolded and tied up her and her foreman with lamp wires in order to steal the famous Krupp diamond in a sensational, highly publicized crime. She had constantly worn the ring, featuring the huge blue-white diamond and its adjacent two baguette diamonds, which was now torn off her finger. The criminals got away with the ring, about $700 thousand cash, a revolver, and a camera. They were captured in New Jersey about six weeks later, after which the diamonds (which had been divided and secretly put up for sale in St. Louis and in New Jersey) were recovered and returned to the ring's distraught owner. The living room where she had been terrorized and robbed is now the visitor center for the property.

Vera Hossenfeldt had been married three times before marrying Krupp, first to a German baron, then an aspiring movie producer, then a doctor. In his book *The Arms of Krupp*, William Manchester termed the beautiful Vera "a charter member of the jet set." Krupp, the wealthiest industrialist in Germany, was reportedly obsessed with her and devastated when she filed for divorce.

It would be nice to imagine that Vera divorced him because he had overseen concentration camps using slave labor, as well as a camp for the laborers' children under the age of two. Or because he was the main financier of Hitler's election campaign for Chancellor in 1932. Or because he built tanks and other military equipment for Hitler. Or because he was a member of the elite Nazi SS troops. Or because he was convicted of war crimes and jailed until 1951 on those charges. From most accounts, though, she was just bored with him and missed her former lifestyle in the sunny American West.

When she left Europe and moved to Vegas, she invested approximately $70 thousand in a luxury hotel and casino, which soon became bankrupt and owed a substantial amount of back taxes. The relative peace and quiet of the ranch—except for the robbery, of course—must have been soothing after such a big loss to her bank account and her pride. The Baroness became a competent cattle rancher, raising a hybrid strain of Brahma and white-faced Hereford on the century-old ranch.

Original settler Bill Williams' 1864 cabin and blacksmith's shop (some of the oldest structures in the valley near Vegas) still are available for tours, along with the Baroness' own luxurious ranch home. Entertainment is offered to today's visitors via a living history program about Las Vegas' pioneers, demonstrations of early pioneer skills, the Super Summer Theatre series, and the Theatre Under the Stars musicals and plays.

The Frau Vera Hossenfeldt von Langer Wisbar Kanuer Krupp von Bohlen und Halbach sold her ranch to Howard Hughes when he started buying up lots of Vegas properties in 1967. The State of Nevada obtained the ranch and all its acreage in 1974, when it became a Nevada state park. It is in the Red Rock Canyon National Conservation Area, and her former home is open for tours. Public concerts also are held here each summer, adding to its attraction for visitors.

The Baroness may have sold the ranch and then passed away on October 16, 1974, but that doesn't mean she left the Spring Mountain Ranch permanently. Her glamorously attired ghost has been seen wandering around her former home, especially her bedroom and closet area, by quite a few visitors. Of the many houses, and even mansions where she resided during her lifetime, apparently this is the one where Vera Krupp still feels the most at home.

7

FRANK SINATRA

To many people, Frank Sinatra is synonymous with Las Vegas. As an in-demand performer at its glamorous clubs (beginning with a 1951 debut at the Desert Inn) and the acknowledged leader of the Rat Pack, he was a major and greatly respected force in the city. With movies like *Ocean's Eleven*, filmed at the Sands with his pals, he helped focus international attention on the Vegas Strip and its many attractions. He even recorded the hit live album *Sinatra at the Sands*, in 1966 in Vegas with the Count Basie Band, arranged by Quincy Jones.

Born Francis Albert Sinatra to Italian immigrants, the charismatic vocalist was a star ever since he began singing with Harry James' band at the tender age of twenty-four. In just under a year, he'd shot up to singing for Tommy Dorsey's extraordinarily popular band. He quickly became the object of the adoration of swooning, screaming, fanatical teenage girl "bobby soxers," and his rise from that point was meteoric.

Termed "the Voice," he went solo and soon became a movie star, joining Gene Kelly at the top of the bill in the hit *Anchors Aweigh*. He later earned an Academy Award for Best Supporting Actor for his acting in the role of Maggio in *From Here to Eternity* and was a finalist for Best Actor for his performance in *The Man with the Golden Arm*.

All his life, Sinatra was friendly to and supported by mobsters. It's understandable that he would be appreciative to the ones—like Sam "Mo-Mo" Giancana (head of the Chicago Outfit and believed to be a gunman at the St. Valentine's Day Massacre), Willie Moretti (at whose daughter's wedding Sinatra sang), and Paul "Skinny" D'Amato, who gave him singing jobs early on at their nightclubs—but it went further than that. All the way back to Italy, in fact. Sinatra's father's family and the family of gangster extraordinaire Salvatore Luciana, more commonly known as "Lucky" Luciano (often called the founder of the modern Mafia), lived on the very same street in their hometown of Lercara Friddi on the Italian island of Sicily. Luciano's parents and Sinatra's grandparents were married at the same church, Santa Maria della Neve. This, perhaps not so coincidentally, was only a few miles from the towns of Corleone and Prizzi, which were known homes of the Mafia. So there was nothing odd or particularly scary (usually) to Sinatra at being around Mafia-type figures.

He grew up in a tough neighborhood in Hoboken, New Jersey, with an equally tough family. Members of Sinatra's own family were bootleggers when he was just a boy, and his mother, Dolly, was convicted of performing abortions as a side-role to her career as a midwife. His uncle Lawrence "Babe" Garavente served prison time for murder before moving in with the Sinatras for a few years. His neighbors, the Fischetti family, were especially friendly with Frank and his parents. Two of the sons (Rocco and Charles) later worked closely with Al Capone, who was their cousin. Their brother, Joe "Stingy" Fischetti, would be a good friend and long-time business associate of Sinatra.

Sinatra first sang publicly at the age of eleven in his parents' tavern, Marty O'Brien's, which had been named in honor of the alias used by his father when he boxed. Marty and Dolly's business was protected by gangsters, and Marty himself helped ensure other liquor shipments weren't hijacked by competitors. Frank dropped out of high school and then left home for New York at seventeen. After a few years without a major break, he returned home and got a job, it is said with the help of mobster Angelo "Gyp" DeCarlo, serving as a waiter and a singer at the popular Rustic Cabin club. He also had performed to raves at Moretti's Riviera on the Jersey Palisades across from Manhattan. For years after the Depression, if entertainers wanted to work, they usually had to work for mob-owned clubs because they were primarily the only ones with money to keep them open.

Police and Bureau of Narcotics documents later claimed that Sinatra was discovered by Mafia "biggies" Moretti, Frank Costello, and Luciano. He got his job with Harry James' band on his own, though, and it was with that band that he made his first commercial recordings. James graciously allowed him to join Dorsey's orchestra in 1940, and that's when Sinatra became an almost immediate smash with the audiences. He also recorded eighty-four songs with Dorsey during the roughly three years he performed with him. "I'll Never Smile Again" became his first big hit.

When Sinatra wanted to leave Dorsey for a solo career two years before the expiration of their contract, Dorsey angrily resisted. Then he agreed, but wanted to force Sinatra to pay a huge percentage of his future income to him, perhaps indefinitely. (Sinatra later said Dorsey wanted one third of his income for the rest of his life.) So Sinatra allegedly got a little help from his friends, who persuaded Dorsey to let him go without the monetary conditions when they (in alternate versions provided later by Sinatra, Dorsey, or Dorsey's friends) told Dorsey he'd no longer perform on radio, pulled a gun on him, and/or threatened to kidnap his children.

Luciano himself later gave a further reason why Sinatra was indebted to the mob. He said they'd pumped money (up to about $60 thousand) into Sinatra's career when he became a solo act to make sure he'd become the star they knew he had the talent to be.

His Oscar award-winning role (1953s Academy Award for Best Supporting Actor) in *From Here to Eternity* was said to be another gift from his Mafia friends. Columbia's studio head Harry Cohn hated Sinatra and refused to sign him for the role of Maggio, though Sinatra had tested magnificently. Cohn allegedly was quite convincingly coerced by threats against his life by mobsters. Suddenly, Cohn agreed that Sinatra was the ideal actor to play the role. Of course, once he landed the role, Sinatra was so perfect that it brought his career to a whole new level.

Sinatra became a huge asset to the mob when he helped popularize the Sands Hotel and Casino, which mobsters—

including Frank Costello and Giancana—secretly owned. Sinatra, who himself owned an interest (he bought two percent, while seven percent was a gift) in the venture, was at the grand opening in 1953, and performed there each year until late in the sixties. His shows there with the Rat Pack were a predominant reason Vegas became known as the Entertainment Capital of America, as well as the gambling capital.

Sinatra helped the mob in other ways, according to published reports in magazines and books. He performed a special Christmas Eve concert in 1946 for Luciano, who was in exile in Cuba. Just two months later, he allegedly acted on February 11, 1947 as a money courier for $2 million from American mobsters to Luciano. His traveling companions when he flew to Havana for the four days in February were old friends and known mobsters Joe and Rocco Fischetti. He was photographed with Luciano at a Havana nightclub, on the balcony at the Hotel Nacional and in poses with the Fischetti brothers and Luciano. Written reports even stated he had been involved in an orgy in Havana with various mobsters and a dozen call-girls—which supposedly had been interrupted by a troop of Girl Scouts led by a shocked nun, who immediately hustled the innocent young Scouts out of the room.

During these trips to Cuba, Sinatra wasn't involved, however, with the mobsters' business meetings, at which they discussed a hit on Benny Siegel and the takeover of his Flamingo Hotel & Casino. Sinatra was an admirer of Siegel, and even went with trusted friends—just days after the gangster's eventual murder—to the very room in California where he'd been killed in order to toast his memory.

Sinatra paid court to Luciano again when he traveled to Naples, Italy, to visit the exiled Mafia boss, even giving him a gold engraved cigarette case and his unlisted phone number.

Even as late as 1966, comedian Jackie Mason was threatened by the mob when he made jokes about Sinatra and his then-wife Mia Farrow in his Vegas act. Refusing to stop the insulting jokes despite phone threats, death threats, and shots fired into his hotel room in Vegas, Mason finally got the message after a thug with brass knuckles broke his nose and smashed his cheekbone, telling Mason, "We warned you to stop using the Sinatra material in your act." Some people just won't take a hint.

Despite their mutual favors to each other, Sinatra's relationship to mobsters—called "The Boys" in Vegas—cost him dearly. Sinatra lost his license from the Nevada State Gaming Control Board after the FBI realized Giancana had secretly stayed more than eleven days at Lake Tahoe's Cal-Neva Lodge, at which Sinatra was more than fifty percent owner, with Sinatra's full knowledge. (Dean Martin had been a partner, but luckily gave up his interest in the casino/hotel on the border of Nevada and California because of his worries when he first found out about Giancana's presence there, according to Martin's daughter Deana in her book *Memories Are Made Of This: Dean Martin Through His Daughter's Eyes*.) Because he was blacklisted by the government, Giancana legally wasn't allowed to enter any of Nevada's casinos, or even dine in one of their restaurants, much less stay at a Nevada hotel casino resort for several days. When the Gaming Control Board began investigating the situation, Sinatra was recorded in a call angrily threatening the chief investigator. He had the agents kicked out of the Cal-Neva, and then D'Amato attempted to bribe them. When Sinatra realized he couldn't beat the charges, he reluctantly divested himself of his interests in both the Cal-Neva and in the Sands (of which he at one time owned nine percent—two he had bought himself and seven that were a gift from Vicente "Jimmy Blue Eyes" Alo).

Though losing his license and his casino interests was financially harmful and publicly humiliating, more personally heartbreaking to Sinatra was the withdrawal of President John F. Kennedy's friendship, allegedly due to Sinatra's associations with mobsters—even though many claim both Sinatra and the mob had played a huge role in his winning the Presidential election in 1960, supposedly at the urging and full knowledge of Kennedy's father, Joe. Joe Kennedy himself had made his fortune bootlegging whisky during Prohibition, and he allegedly felt no compunction or guilt about using his connections to help his son become President (by reportedly pressuring voters at the polls and buying votes in Chicago, for example).

In a 2000 interview on television's *60 Minutes*, Sinatra's daughter, Tina, admitted that he had acquiesced to Joe Kennedy's request that he intercede with Giancana for help in obtaining union votes for Jack Kennedy's presidential campaign. She added that her father had taken responsibility himself with a furious Giancana when the Kennedy administration cracked down on the mob instead of taking it easy on them as the Kennedy patriarch had indicated before the election. She quoted Giancana as saying that Joe Kennedy owed him, with Sinatra correcting him, "No, I owe you. I asked for the favor." She said that, in an effort to make it up to him, Sinatra had brought Martin and Davis with him to play, at no cost to Giancana, eight nights of twice-daily shows at the mobster's Villa Venice club in Chicago.

The loyal Sinatra had believed his home would become an unofficial West Coast White House, so he was devastated when President Kennedy let him know, through Lawford (whom Sinatra had called "brother-in-lawford), that he would stay at Bing Crosby's home instead of Sinatra's on a visit to Palm Springs on March 24, 1961. The president, after all, understandably couldn't sleep in the very same room where mobster Giancana had stayed on previous visits to Sinatra's home. Sinatra had excitedly (and expensively) redecorated every room in his home (except his own bedroom), built two cottages for Secret Service agents, installed a helicopter pad and special phone system and put up a flagpole like he had seen at the president's home at Hyannis Port in anticipation of the president's stay. Upon his receipt of the phone call, a shocked Sinatra went outside with a jackhammer and personally destroyed the helipad.

Sinatra was so angry at this rejection that he cut Lawford out of the Rat Pack and his life, blaming him and the president's brother, Bobby, instead of the president himself. Probably he never found out that the impetus for this insult had come from the FBI's J. Edgar Hoover, who firmly let the Kennedys know they had to drop their association with Sinatra. He made sure they knew he was aware of the relationship between the president, Sinatra, Giancana, and their mutual lover, Judith Campbell, an association that could destroy the Kennedy's presidency and the future of his family if it were public knowledge. (Sinatra had first introduced Kennedy and Giancana to Campbell in Vegas.) If Sinatra had been told of the threat by Hoover, made just two days before the planned stay at Sinatra's home, it may have made a huge difference in his reaction.

Reportedly, Sinatra had been the personal intermediary, at the request of Joe Kennedy, who gained the support—and help in the campaign, both monetarily and otherwise—of Giancana, D'Amato, Tommy Lucchese, and other top mobsters. Sinatra also campaigned his heart out, playing at fund-raisers for the Democratic candidate and convincing his Hollywood friends to contribute their time and donations for the cause. He even supplied private airplanes to transport stars to rallies and other events for Kennedy. He also provided free records of his campaign song for JFK (a reworking of "High Hopes") to each of the delegates at the Democratic convention in Los Angeles, just a little personal enticement to name Kennedy as the party's candidate for the highest office in the land.

The newly-elected President Kennedy shocked the country's normally cynical mobsters when he named their nemesis, his brother Robert "Bobby" Kennedy, as the U.S. Attorney General. Bobby had pledged for years to bring down Giancana and other organized crime figures. When he was chief counsel of the Senate Subcommittee on Investigations, Bobby had personally interrogated Giancana, who absolutely hated him, though the mob don had given his full support to Bobby's brother.

The mob felt betrayed by the Kennedys and, by extension, Sinatra, who was said to have been threatened himself by Giancana. Though Giancana and Sinatra reconciled on the surface, continuing their social and professional association, dining together and visiting each other's homes, Giancana was said to have told others that he sporadically considered putting a hit out on Sinatra until the violent end of his own life in 1975.

Despite his bitter disappointment at being dumped by the Kennedy family, Sinatra remained a great admirer of President Kennedy and was devastated by his assassination. About two weeks later, his son, Frank Jr., was kidnapped. Though the novice kidnappers were captured and jailed, Frank Jr. said in his court testimony that he thought from their comments that the plan had been conceived by "higher-ups in organized crime." His sister, Tina Sinatra, later admitted that their father feared the kidnapping had been a warning that he should remain quiet about his suspicions that the mob might have been involved in the Kennedy assassination. Perhaps as a result, he never did publicly give his views on who he thought had killed his friend, the President.

The FBI tried for four decades (and approximately 1,275 pages of documents, the largest file on any entertainer in American history) to prove, without success, that the singer had committed any crimes associated with his various mob connections.

Sinatra, despite his occasional violent outbursts and association with unsavory characters, was known throughout his life for his frequent generous, thoughtful, and compassionate acts not just to family and friends but often to strangers who never even knew he was their benefactor. One example was his gift of a bus to a needy school, on the sole condition that they weren't told who gave them the bus. He quietly took care of friends' medical expenses and even sometimes personally made them tea and toast while they recovered from illnesses. He sent special gold St. Christopher medals to an entire crew of sailors on a PT boat that had been rechristened the *Oh Frankie!* He liked to give expensive gold gifts (Dunhill cigarette lighters, money clips, key chains, and cuff links) to friends, service staff, and even short-term acquaintances. He generously gave both his time and money through the years to various charities, even serving as campaign chairman for the National Sclerosis Society.

His good friend, Ronald Reagan, asked him to produce both of his presidential inaugural galas, just as President Kennedy had done for his inauguration two decades earlier. In 1985, President Reagan awarded Sinatra the highest civilian award in America, the Medal of Freedom. For someone known to value his freedom and indeed to have done it his way all his life, that had to be an especially sweet honor. He also was presented with the Congressional Gold Medal in 1997, and was an honoree at 1983's Kennedy Center Honors.

During his career, he received eleven Grammy Awards, including the Trustees Award and the Lifetime Achievement Award. He was presented with the prestigious Legend Award at the Grammy

Awards show in 1994 after a lengthy tribute by the singer Bono, though producers shamefully cut Sinatra's own speech short to go to commercial. They wouldn't have dared to do that in his glory days.

Sinatra continued through the years to perform in Vegas. He played at the Sands until, under the ownership of Howard Hughes, the casino cut off his credit and he subsequently had an ugly public fight in the Garden Terrace Coffee Shop at the hotel. He threw furniture and hot coffee at casino boss Carl Cohen, who threw a punch that knocked out the bridgework for two of Sinatra's front teeth and busted his lip. Not surprisingly, Sinatra packed up, walked out, and didn't return to the Sands for years. Sinatra and Hughes had grudges against each other, anyway, since Hughes and Sinatra had begun their separate involvements around the same time with the stunning Ava Gardner, so he probably wouldn't have kept performing there with Hughes as owner. Alan King filled in for him during Sinatra's last scheduled shows at the Sands. Within a year, Sinatra had signed a new contract, this time to perform at the luxurious Caesars Palace.

Sinatra hadn't given up on becoming more than an entertainer in Vegas, though. He applied to the Nevada Gaming Control Board for a new license in 1981, and it was easily granted to him in just a few months.

There was a part of the man that was still sentimental about his time at the Sands. Sinatra was very upset when the Sands was demolished in 1996, not approving of that decision at all. In the excellent book *Sinatra: The Life* by Anthony Summers and Robbyn Swan, actor Jerry Lewis was quoted as saying, "Frank took it as a personal affront. He asked, 'How could they do that?'"

Vegas thought of Sinatra as its own, and he certainly had helped bring a certain caché to the city's image throughout the world. When Sinatra passed away in May of 1998, the lights on Vegas' Strip went dark, just as they had at the deaths of his fellow Rat Packers and close pallies, Sammy Davis Jr. and Dean Martin. Thousands on the silent streets held candles in his honor, and when the lights came on again, Caesars Palace sported a giant illuminated likeness of the entertainer. His personality still seems to be imprinted on Vegas, which was definitely the ideal home base for Sinatra and his pals.

8

THE RAT PACK

The coolest of the cool. The swingingest of the swinging. That was the iconic Rat Pack in the early sixties. Frank Sinatra, Dean "Dino" Martin, Sammy Davis Jr., Peter Lawford, and Joey Bishop are the ones who initially come to mind, though Shirley McLaine, Angie Dickinson, Lauren Bacall, Marilyn Monroe, Juliet Prowse, and Judy Garland were unofficially members ("Rat Pack Mascots").

They even had their own lingo, calling squares "Harvey," using "cool" or "crazy" or "cuckoo" to show admiration or approval, calling good times a "gas," and using "clyde" as an all-purpose term. If they liked you, they might call you "Charlie," "chicky baby" or "pally."

This wasn't the first Rat Pack. Sinatra also was in that one—the Holmby Hills Rat Pack. It was a group of friends, loosely led by Humphrey Bogart, who often met at the house (Holmby Hills) of Garland and husband Sid Luft. Bogart's wife, Bacall, was called, affectionately, the Den Mother. Other members of the often hard-drinking group were Katherine Hepburn, Spencer Tracy, Cary Grant, David Niven, Swifty Lazar, Nathaniel Benchley, Jimmy Van Heusen, and, on occasion, Mickey Rooney, Errol Flynn, and Caesar Romero.

The origin of the first group's name is widely debated, sometimes being credited to either columnist Hedda Hopper or Louella Parsons or, most often, to Bacall, who supposedly said the guys looked like "a goddamn rat pack" after they came back from a night of carousing in Vegas. Garland reportedly gave each member a decorative pin featuring a ruby-eyed rat as a memento.

Sinatra actually hated the name Rat Pack, so its members in the later incarnation initially called their group the Clan when they formed it in 1959. Davis joked, in a reference to the Ku Klux Klan, that he wouldn't have belonged to anything named the Clan.

The group's name soon changed to the Summit of Cool or, more often, simply the Summit. Again, the source of the name varies. Some, including Davis, said it was named after the summit meeting of world leaders President Dwight Eisenhower, Nikita Khrushchev, and Charles de Gaulle in Paris, while others recall that it was named after the famous meeting of President John F. Kennedy and Khrushchev. Regardless, the press started calling it the Rat Pack, and that's how most people came to refer to the group of entertainers.

Whether it was called the Summit or the Rat Pack, the group became as legendary for its uproarious ad-libbed humor as for its great music. Martin and Sinatra were arguably the best crooners in the world then (probably ever), with a wicked sense of humor, and the multi-talented Davis, suave Lawford, and sardonically humorous Bishop fit right into the group. They were so close that, when Davis lost an eye in a car accident, Sinatra and Dean both wore eye patches in unspoken support.

If one of the pack was playing in Vegas (famously at the Sands' Copa Room), the others usually turned up to join in the fun. Typical of their sense of anything-can-happen humor, in an often-recalled moment at the Copa Room, Martin even carried Sammy Davis Jr. to the microphone, dryly commenting, "I want to thank the NAACP for this award."

Jack Entratter, entertainment director of the Sands Hotel, had been pallies with Martin since giving him and former partner Jerry Lewis their big break in New York when he managed the famous Copacabana for Frank Costello. Both Martin and

Sinatra even became stockowners of the Sands. Martin was the first entertainer with just one name—DINO— on a marquee in Vegas. Though many think that's a nickname, it actually was his real name (Dino Crocetti). It was at Dino's shows that the Rat Pack first began showing up and joining in onstage. He even was Elvis' stated hero and inspiration, with Elvis terming him "the king of cool."

Naturally, the Rat Pack's shows all sold out, their audiences went wild, and they largely were responsible for gaining Vegas the reputation as entertainment center of the world. The Sands Hotel, well described by its sign that stated "A Place in the Sun," definitely was the place to be in the Swinging Sixties. Sold-out crowds poured into Vegas for the Rat Pack's glamorous, hilariously funny, celebrity-attended shows.

Sinatra and group brought even more free publicity to Vegas and the Sands when the entire Rat Pack filmed the popular, now iconic movie *Ocean's Eleven* there from January 26 to February 16, 1960. (It was one of the top five box office hits in Warner Brothers history.) Sinatra filmed his scenes in only nine days. Because the storyline was set during the Christmas season, there were lavish Christmas decorations all over the areas used for filming, which was a little baffling to tourists who didn't realize at first that it was being used as a movie set.

The Rat Pack performed at the Sands each night after making the movie during the day. Martin, who'd dealt cards in his hometown of Steubenville, Ohio, even surprised the casino's gamblers by occasionally relieving other dealers and taking over a blackjack table at the Sands. Somehow the group also found time to gamble, play poker, hit the golf course, and entertain their famous friends who visited the movie set and took in the entertainers' enormously popular stage shows.

As a presidential candidate, Jack Kennedy even took in a performance while he was in Vegas. The Rat Pack were tremendously dedicated campaigners for Kennedy, who was the brother-in-law of Lawford. They were even called "the Jack Pack" for a while. Sinatra, in particular, was a huge booster of the Democratic candidate, even contributing a theme song to his 1960 campaign. After winning the election, Kennedy (perhaps at the urging of his brother Bobby or more probably because J. Edgar Hoover let Bobby know he finally had figured out the connection between President Kennedy, Giancana, Sinatra, and the woman—Judith Campbell—that those three shared), broke off his relationship with Sinatra because of the singer's connections with members of the Mafia. As a result, the devastated Sinatra blamed Lawford for not intervening with his brother-in-law, immediately cutting Lawford out of the Rat Pack and his life. It was perhaps easier to shift the blame to the hapless Lawford than to admit to himself that his pally Kennedy had deserted him.

The remainder of the group, however, remained tight, continuing to perform in Vegas during the sixties and filming more movies together, including 1962's *Sergeants 3* and 1964's *Robin and the Seven Hoods*. Various members starred in several other movies with each other, ending with the appearances of Martin and Davis in *The Cannonball Run* and Martin, Davis, Sinatra, and Shirley McLaine in *Cannonball Run II*.

In 1967, Howard Hughes bought the Sands, and Sinatra's casino credit was stopped. He and the casino's Carl Cohen had a huge fight, during which the bridgework for two of Sinatra's front teeth was knocked out. So Sinatra left the Sands for a new contract at Caesars Palace. Martin, who had first performed in Vegas in 1949 at the Flamingo with then-partner Jerry Lewis, stayed at the Sands for two more years before he switched over to the Riviera.

The background of the Rat Pack also has brought loud whispers through the years about a connection to the mob. As has often been said, though, mobsters often owned the clubs where they played, employing the entertainers and sometimes socializing with them in the course of that employment. It didn't mean the performers necessarily approved of all their employers' actions, but they of course had a natural gratitude to those who had hired them. Sam Giancano and Paul "Skinny" D'Amato were among those who had friendships of a sort with members of the Rat Pack, which caused FBI surveillance of the entertainers. Martin was one of those checked out, and he was completely exonerated. Sinatra wasn't so lucky, but that's a topic for an earlier chapter.

Missing the Rat Pack's glory days of performing and hanging out together, Sinatra spearheaded the 1987 "Together Again" world tour with Martin and Davis. Martin only stayed around for three performances, replaced by family friend Liza Minnelli, the daughter of original Holmby Hills Rat Packer Garland. He, Sinatra, and Davis remained in contact, though, with their friendships intact for the rest of their lives.

One of the most lasting contributions of the Rat Pack was their refusal to go along with the then-racial segregation in Vegas. Martin and Sinatra, in particular, refused to perform at the Sands unless Davis was allowed to sleep and eat there. Though they made jokes onstage about each other's heritage, they wouldn't allow anyone to treat them unequally. Their close friendship and constant inclusion of Davis onstage and off proved such a strong example that it was a big factor in breaking the back of segregation there. Appropriately, in 1972, Davis became the first African American to become an owner of a Vegas Strip hotel when he bought eight percent of the Tropicana.

Though all the Rat Pack have passed on, their memory is still strong in Vegas and beyond. At their deaths, Davis and Martin were the first two entertainers for whom Vegas' Strip paid the tribute of turning off its constantly burning bright lights, with only the flickering candlelight of their grieving admirers breaking through the darkness. At Sinatra's death, the lights went out again, coming on minutes later to reveal the singer's huge likeness lit up on Caesars Palace.

The legislature of his home state of Ohio even honored Martin in 2002 by declaring his birthdate of June 7th to be a state holiday, Dean Martin Day, from that point on. He was the first American entertainer to have had a holiday named in his honor.

"The Rat Pack Is Back: The Tribute to Frank, Sammy, Joey, and Dean" has been very popular in this decade, with daily shows at the city's Plaza Hotel and Casino Plaza Theater. Newly packaged live concert albums by the sixties Rat Pack themselves were well-received when they were released from 1999-2004. The 1998 television movie *The Rat Pack*, starring Joe Mantegna, Ray Liotta, Don Cheadle, Angus Macfadyen, Bobby Slayton, and William Petersen, told the group's story to a new generation. Prestigious actors George Clooney, Brad Pitt, Julia Roberts, Matt Damon, Cheadle, Andy Garcia, Carl Reiner, Bernie Mac, Catherine Zeta Zones, Al Pacino, and Ellen Barkin filmed a series of popular "Oceans" movies (*Ocean's Eleven*, *Ocean's Twelve*, and *Ocean's Thirteen*) about four decades after the original *Oceans Eleven*.

The Sands was demolished on November 26, 1996, but it lives on in the Rat Pack's movies and music. Who knows—perhaps the spirits of Sinatra, Martin, Davis, Lawford, and Bishop themselves are still lingering in the city they so personified. Certainly, the hip aura created by the strong personalities of the legendary entertainers lives on every day—and especially during the glittering nights—in Vegas.

9

MARILYN

Marilyn Monroe was probably the greatest female sex symbol of the twentieth century. With starring roles in movies like *Gentlemen Prefer Blondes, Some Like It Hot* (for which she won a Golden Globe award), *The Misfits* (filmed in the desert near Vegas), *Bus Stop, The Seven Year Itch*, and *River of No Return*, she became one of the most famous actresses in the world. Sadly, fame and the adoration of movie-goers didn't translate to a happy love life or her personal self-confidence off the screen. Because of that, the stunning star often was a victim of the various private agendas and sexual greed of those who later deserted and betrayed her.

Reportedly romantically involved with Frank Sinatra every now and then, Monroe was close to the members of the Rat Pack and enjoyed being in the audience at their shows in Vegas. Her beloved poodle, named Maf (short for "Mafia"), was a gift from Sinatra. Dean Martin was such a loyal friend to her that he refused to go on filming the movie *Something's Got to Give*, when she was temporarily fired from the production and there was brief talk of replacing her. Monroe was rehired but had not yet resumed filming for the movie before her death at the tragically young age of thirty-six.

Sinatra and fellow Rat Packer Peter Lawford, didn't really do her any favors, though, by helping in her hookups with Lawford's brothers-in-law, President John Kennedy and then Attorney

General Bobby Kennedy. She and then presidential candidate Kennedy allegedly were intimate in Vegas, Los Angeles, and New York, often with the complicity of Lawford and Sinatra. When his brother, Bobby, told her that President Kennedy had called off his relationship with her, Monroe and Bobby reportedly became involved romantically themselves.

On July 27-29, 1962 (less than two weeks before she died), Marilyn is said to have hung out with Sinatra, Lawford, and Chicago mob don Sam Giancana at the Sinatra and mob-owned Cal-Neva Lodge at Lake Tahoe, Nevada. As always, she stayed in Cabin 3, which connected through a tunnel with Cabin 5, only used by Sinatra or one of the Kennedy brothers. Sources have said that she and Giancana each admitted to friends the surprising news that they even had a sexual encounter that weekend, though other reports said the two did not like each other. Marilyn reportedly overdosed while at the Cal-Neva Lodge, but she survived; it was hushed up, and she returned to Los Angeles. Sinatra supposedly took what could have been considered compromising photos of the intoxicated and drugged-up star that weekend but an upset Sinatra burned them after her death on August 5, 1962, in order to protect Marilyn's memory.

Since her mysterious death on August 4, 1962, in her Los Angeles home, the purported real reason the cultural icon perished has been postulated, rumored, studied, and written about by countless friends, law enforcement, reporters, medical examiners, authors, and fans. The official cause of death was "probable suicide," though many then and now think that was a cover-up of the truth—that Marilyn was murdered for reasons that may not have really been about her.

Evidence has since shown that her home at 12305 Fifth Helena Drive in the Brentwood area of L.A. was wire-tapped, reportedly by J. Edgar Hoover and the FBI, the CIA, National Teamsters Union president Jimmy Hoffa, and Giancana. When the house was remodeled after its purchase by actress Victoria Hamel and her husband in 1972, a "standard FBI issue" phone tap and eavesdropping system covering the entire house was uncovered. All of these listening devices are believed to have been monitored for use to either destroy, blackmail, or protect the Kennedy brothers, depending on the listener's own agenda. Hoover wanted the upper hand over the Kennedys or—at the very least—not to be fired by them. The CIA was angry about the Bay of Pigs fiasco, for which they blamed the President. Hoffa and Giancana were convinced Monroe knew too much, and they would have loved to use private information to stop the Attorney General in his tracks as he continued with his dogged attempt to shut down the mob and also end Hoffa's influence. Many believe, though, that one or more of the above went much further than listening in on Monroe.

The scenarios about her death that are presented in various books (over 600 have been written about Marilyn's life) are chilling, especially since they often seem all too plausible. One theory is that the mob orchestrated Monroe's murder in order to frame the Kennedys. According to this idea, Marilyn had become pregnant and aborted Bobby's baby, at his insistence, at which point he unceremoniously dumped her. She supposedly threatened to hold a press conference telling all the details about her relationships with the brothers. In that era, it would effectively have ended the Kennedy era, so the theory called for the Kennedys to be blamed, even though the mob would actually have been the ones who planned and carried out the hit on the blonde superstar.

Giancana and his fellow gangsters were supposed to have poured a lot of cash ($1 million from Giancana himself) and muscle (especially in the Chicago area) into the campaign to have Kennedy elected President, then Kennedy didn't follow through with what they had understood would be protection of the mob from the Justice Department's harassment and arrests. So their revenge would be the destruction of the Kennedys by making sure their involvement with Marilyn came out and they were blamed for her murder.

Another idea is that the CIA murdered Monroe, again in order to blame and thus ruin the Kennedys. Or that it was a joint effort between the CIA and the mob, who shared a common goal of wanting the brothers out of office.

What most of the scenarios have in common is that Monroe did not commit suicide but rather was sedated by chloryl hydrate, then murdered by a massive dose of barbiturates administered to a helpless Monroe through an enema. This was borne out by her autopsy results, though her tissue and fluid samples mysteriously disappeared, as did most of the originally thick police file on the Monroe case. Chief of Police William Parker was said to have brought the majority of the file to Attorney General Kennedy as part of a cover-up performed to make sure the Kennedys were not framed for the death by the real murderers.

Lawford also was supposed to have participated in the cover-up, ensuring that Monroe's house was swept clean of any evidence that might have been incriminating to the Kennedy family. The Attorney General himself was allegedly at the house earlier in the day to meet with Marilyn and try unsuccessfully to convince her to turn over her diary (said to have confidential state secrets confided to her by Bobby) and other paperwork (and maybe even a photo of President Kennedy with Giancana). If any such evidence was in the house earlier that day, it was gone within hours after Marilyn's death.

Sergeant Jack Clemmons, present at the house that night, always felt Monroe had been murdered. He saw no glass by the bed, and she was known to be incapable of swallowing pills without water (or sometimes champagne); and he thought it odd that the washing machine and vacuum cleaner were going strong in the middle of the night. The prescription bottles at the bedside were empty, though they were partially full later and a drinking glass also magically appeared by the bed.

Her friends in the Rat Pack, especially Martin, Sinatra, and Lawford, were said to have been very shaken by her death. They attempted to attend her funeral, but were banned—as were the entire Kennedy family and her other Hollywood friends—by Marilyn's ex-husband, Joe DiMaggio, who took charge of the funeral and kept away those he considered had been bad influences or who may contributed in any way to her death.

Though they had divorced, DiMaggio still loved her and knew that, despite any appearances to the contrary, Marilyn wasn't the dumb, shallow blonde that many in the public believed her to be. Her IQ was 168 (18 points above that considered to be highly gifted), she loved to read good literature (with more than 400 books on a wide variety of subjects in her own library), she was loyal to her friends, and had successfully studied with some of the acting world's greatest coaches. Sadly, though, her abandonment as a child, her fear of inheriting her mother's insanity, her inability to stay happily married, and her almost constant struggle to be taken seriously in her profession as an actress lent themselves to her lifelong insecurities, and lack of self-respect.

Decades later, the public's fascination with the vulnerable actress hasn't abated. The woman who appeared in 1953 on the first cover of *Playboy* magazine was voted the Sexiest Woman of the Century nearly half a century later in 1999 by *People Magazine*. She was the subject of the U. S. Post Office's first stamp in the Legends of Hollywood series in 1995.

Though Monroe isn't generally thought of in terms of her time in Vegas, it was said to have been the scene of happy times for her, and numerous visitors are said to have sighted her ghost wandering through the hotels where she had partied with her friends. Others have said that they have seen her spirit at the Cal-Neva Lodge, where she had spent time with Sinatra, Peter and Pat Lawford, and, allegedly, John or Bobby Kennedy.

10

LIBERACE & CARLUCCIO'S TIVOLI GARDENS

With a trademark candelabra artfully placed on top of his piano, Wladziu Valentino Liberace, known simply as Liberace, played to throngs of adoring fan worldwide. His showy piano prowess was often panned by critics, but the fans never noticed. Although an extremely proficient player, who earned a scholarship to the Wisconsin Conservatory of Music at the age of seven, it was his showmanship that captivated the crowds; he was a flashy, ludicrously funny, very kind, and often misunderstood man.

Liberace began his superstar run in the early 1950s and averaged $5 million a year for more than thirty-five years. The *1978 Guinness Book of World Records* identified Liberace as the world's highest paid musician. In the 1940s, he began playing extended runs in Las Vegas, starting in 1944 at the Last Frontier Hotel. He would appear up and down the Strip in showrooms including not only The Last Frontier, but The Riviera, The Aladdin, the Sahara, the El Cortez, the original MGM Grand, Caesars Palace, and the Las Vegas Hilton, performing on a regular basis for the rest of his life.

In 1978, Liberace built his own museum to allow fans a glimpse of his personal life and past. It also gave him a place to showcase his opulent collections. The museum contains many of Liberace's extravagant cars, a gold casting of Liberace's hands, dozens of

The Liberace Museum. *Photo by Liz Cavanaugh.*

candelabra, a painting of his mother, a rotating rhinestone-covered piano, the multi-million dollar stage wardrobe (including his famous red, white, and blue sequined hot pants), his collection of rare and antique pianos, glittering stage jewelry, and the world's largest rhinestone. Twenty years later, the Liberace Museum and gift shop remains one of the most popular tourist attractions in Las Vegas.

In 1982, Liberace purchased a restaurant in the strip mall next to his museum. The following year, after lavish renovations, "Liberace's Tivoli Gardens" opened its doors. The fine Italian restaurant's popularity quickly grew, and it soon became a hangout for the stars after they finished their Strip shows. Occasionally, you would catch Liberace tweaking a dish in the kitchen for himself or friends or find him seated at the mirrored piano in the bar entertaining customers. After Liberace's death in 1987, the restaurant was sold and renamed "Carluccio's Tivoli Gardens." The interior remains the same as it did when Liberace owned it.

There are many stories about ghost sightings at the restaurant. A longtime bartender once made a flip remark about the former

Liberace Plaza on Tropicana Avenue. *Photo by Liz Cavanaugh.*

Carluccio's Tivoli Gardens, restaurant formerly owned by Liberace.
Photo by Liz Cavanaugh.

owner, only to have to duck liquor bottles flying off the shelves. Another story goes that the restaurant was having problems with the lights flashing one evening and finally going out. No one could figure out what was causing the problem, until a savvy customer realized that it was Liberace's birthday. Once the crowd and staff finished their raucous rendition of *Happy Birthday*, the lights came back on. The next day, electricians were called to check for possible wiring problems, but none were found. Liberace's theme song was "I'll Be Seeing You (In All the Old Familiar Places)." Apparently, he wasn't kidding.

The wonderful mirrored piano, which was once in Liberace's Vegas home, has occasionally been known to play by itself. The restaurant's mirrored interior provides many guests a first-hand

73

opportunity to catch a glimpse of a white cape (something Liberace frequently used in his stage shows) flashing by. Sinks in the ladies' bathroom have a mind of their own; lights are known to turn on and

off; objects occasionally move around by unseen forces, and, more then once, unsuspecting patrons of the ladies room have heard the door latch mysteriously click and found themselves locked in.

Known as Mr. Showmanship, Liberace owned several homes, including an elaborate mansion in Vegas boasting twenty rooms, two kitchens, six bathrooms, and a sunken marble bathtub. Painted ceilings, a mini version of the Dancing Waters in the back garden, and as a piano-shaped pool made the property one of a kind. Neighbors, after his death, frequently complained that they could hear piano playing, coming from the unoccupied house, at all hours of the night.

The management and staff at Carluccio's are friendly, attentive, more than happy to share stories about their former owner, and even show you a few ghostly photos. The food is also worth the trip off the Strip. The Museum is a fascinating place if you want to kill a couple of hours. Make sure to stay and catch the excellent Liberace tribute show performed by Wes Winter. Winter is charming and funny and does a dead-on Liberace in a campy, but respectful way. It's easy to get

Carluccio's front entrance at night, with orb. *Photo by Liz Cavanaugh.*

caught up in the fun and find yourself singing along to the "Beer Barrel Polka." Again, the management and staff go out of their way to make sure you enjoy your tour. If you're in a wheelchair, you'll get in free. In the later years of her life, Liberace's beloved mother was in a wheelchair, and he made this policy as a tribute to her. The gift shop is full of fun, campy Liberace gifts and souvenirs.

The museum complex also houses the Liberace Foundation, whose mission is to help talented students pursue careers in the performing and creative arts through scholarship assistance. Liberace never forgot his debt to his own scholarships. Today, the Liberace Foundation continues to ensure that hundreds of other gifted young people benefit, as Liberace did in his early days, from such a gift. The Milwaukee Conservatory, today known as The Wisconsin Conservatory of Music, was among the first beneficiaries of his non-profit foundation.

Liberace took his final bow at Radio City Music Hall in New York City on November 2, 1986. His final television appearance was on Christmas Day that same year on *The Oprah Winfrey Show.*

Main entrance to Carluccio's. *Photo by Liz Cavanaugh.*

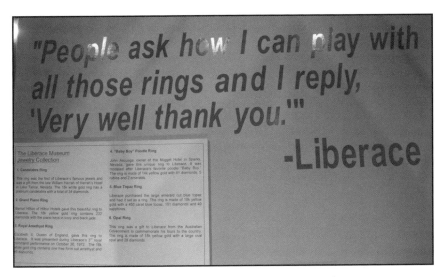

Liberace's favorite line to his audiences. *Photo by Liz Cavanaugh.*

On February 4, 1987, Liberace passed away; he was just sixty-seven years old. He died in his beloved Palm Springs, California, home due to complications from AIDS. His longtime, steadfast manager, Seymour Heller, attributed the star's obvious recent weight loss to a "watermelon diet." But Liberace had been in poor health for a couple of years with problems that included emphysema, as well as heart and liver problems. Exactly when Liberace acquired the virus and became HIV-positive has never been determined.

Volumes have been written about the life of Liberace, some by fans and some by critics, at least one by a scorned lover, and a couple by Liberace himself. By all accounts, he was a wonderful, generous man who loved his fans and lived to entertain. After Liberace's death, Wayne Newton paid tribute to the star saying, "It really doesn't matter how it ends for any of us. The only thing that truly matters are the hearts and souls we touch along the way and Liberace touched many hearts." Amen.

11

HAS ELVIS REALLY
LEFT THE BUILDING?

For so many people, the name Elvis Presley is synonymous with Las Vegas. It is a town where, at any given time, you can see an Elvis impersonator strolling down the street, or eat a fried peanut butter and banana sandwich at any one of several restaurants, or strike up a pose with a frighteningly real likeness of the King of Rock and Roll at Madame Tussaud's Interactive Wax Museum.

If that's not enough, you can head back to the Strip with your sweetie and get hitched at the Viva Las Vegas Wedding Chapel or the Graceland Wedding Chapel. If you don't want the King actually performing your ceremony, you can just have him walk you down the aisle at the Las Vegas Hilton, where they offer Viva Las Vegas and Blue Hawaii wedding packages. As a matter of fact, most area hotels have some sort of Elvis themed wedding package available. Elvis is still big business.

Do you want more Elvis? Look up, you might catch a "Flying Elvis" dropping out of the sky on your way to buy a two-headed velvet Elvis pillow to take home as a souvenir. If you're feeling lucky, you can saddle up to one of several different types of Elvis slot machines around the town and try your luck. It's Las Vegas and the King is still "showing up" everywhere.

The Las Vegas Hilton, formerly known as the International Hotel, opened her doors as an official Hilton property in 1971. The hotel,

LAS VEGAS HILTON SIGN ON PARADISE AVENUE. *PHOTO BY LIZ CAVANAUGH.*

Las Vegas Hilton, where the top floor suite was Elvis' home away from home.
Photo by Liz Cavanaugh.

located at 3000 Paradise Road, was designed by architect Martin Stern, Jr. and originally built in 1969 by Kirk Kerkorian. Like so many other Vegas properties, on the day it opened its doors, it was the largest hotel in the world. Barbra Streisand was the showroom's superstar headliner on opening night, and Peggy Lee performed later that evening in the hotel's lounge. It was Las Vegas in all her razzle-dazzle best.

Although Streisand's performance was a major financial success for the property, it paled by comparison to the King's run that same year. Elvis performed fifty-eight consecutive sold-out shows, breaking all Vegas attendance records, with stellar reviews coming from both critics, and the fans. Elvis's show consisted of new arrangements of his biggest hits, as well as cover hits from other performers. He assembled a group of top-notch rock-n-roll musicians, a full orchestra, white male and black female gospel/soul back-up singers, and an elaborate collection of white jumpsuits to dazzle the crowds.

Elvis broke his own attendance record in February 1970, and again in August 1970 and August 1972. While playing Las Vegas, he lived in the hotel's penthouse suite located on the 30th floor. It was his home away from home until his last performance there in December 1976. Elvis loved Las Vegas, and Las Vegas loved him right back.

Elvis Presley died at his home in Memphis, Tennessee, on August 16, 1977. There are people who think he is still alive and that his death was all an elaborate hoax devised by the King himself so that he could live out the rest of his life anonymously in peace and quiet. As much as his millions of fans around the world would like to believe this, it sadly isn't true.

Fast forward four years to February 10, 1981. Just ninety days after the devastating MGM Grand fire, an arson fire started at the Hilton while it was being retrofitted with modern fire safety equipment. Fast thinking firefighters, using the knowledge they had learned from the MGM fire, used local television networks to notify people to stay in their rooms and avoid going out to the halls and stairwells. Because of the lessons learned, only eight people died in this fire compared with the eighty-five who died in the MGM Grand fire.

Do the ghosts of the eight guests that died haunt the hallowed halls of the Las Vegas Hilton? There have been no reports that they do. The only resident ghost, so it seems, is Mr. Presley. The ghost of Elvis is said to haunt an area around the backstage elevators. Many people have claimed to see an apparition of the King walking around the wings of the showroom and, most frequently, around the elevators which the stage performers use. One frequently told story involves a former maid at the Hilton who routinely rode the elevator each day. Going about her usual business, she stepped on the elevator one morning with her supply cart. She politely said, "Hello, Mr. Presley" as she had many times before. Suddenly, she realized what she had said and who it was that she saw riding along with her. She stopped the elevator, ran out, and never returned to the hotel. Although the ghost of Elvis simply smiled and said "hello" back to her, she was traumatized when she realized that she had indeed seen a ghost.

The Las Vegas Hilton is located off the strip and caters to a more business crowd, connecting you directly to the Las Vegas Convention Center. Its recent renovation has transformed the property into a destination hotel with high-end shopping, fine restaurants, and a spa. The 74,000 square foot casino is state of the art. From 1998 to 2008, visitors could take the "live long and prosper route," slipping away to another galaxy via the Star Trek Museum, with its multitude of costumes and memorabilia. The Star Trek Experience interactive attraction and Quark's Bar and Restaurant are moving to the Neonopolis Mall, a 250,000-square foot shopping mall in downtown Vegas. There are enough shows and entertainment options at the hotel to keep anyone entertained; besides, who knows, you just might see "The King" yourself.

The hotel has been used in the filming of several movies. In 1992, Robert Redford, Demi Moore, and Woody Harrelson filmed *Indecent Proposal* and featured the hotel in several scenes. Extra security had to be brought in to control the crowds of love-struck female fans who flocked to the hotel to catch a glimpse of Mr. Redford. Today, Barry Manilow holds court in the showroom. Following a successful three-year run of sold-out shows, Manilow has recently re-signed to continue with a new show called "Ultimate Manilow, The Hits."

The Hilton is still known for bringing in the biggest headliners in the business to perform in their entertainment venues. Although The King hasn't performed there in many years, he's still an undeniable part of the hotel's history. On August, 16, 2008, a new bronze statue of Elvis was placed near the entrance of the hotel to commemorate the thirty-first anniversary of his passing. There's also another larger statue of him inside.

According to some industry estimates, Elvis Presley has sold more than a billion records worldwide. That's more than any other act in recorded history. He broke all attendance records at the Hilton, and brought in more all-around revenue than any other performer in the hotel's past.

Elvis will always be a part of Las Vegas pop culture. If he still wants to hang around the elevators backstage at the Hilton, he's certainly earned the right. Who knows, maybe The King has become a Barry Manilow fan.

12

REDD FOXX WON'T LEAVE HIS LAS VEGAS HOME

R edd Foxx was a man of many talents. A comedian, actor, and television show host, Foxx was one of the more popular acts to play the clubs and showrooms in Las Vegas. Apparently, Foxx loved living there so much he doesn't want to leave, as numerous reports say he continues to visit his home at Eastern Avenue and Rawhide Street.

The comedian was born in St. Louis, Missouri on December 9, 1922, and named John Elroy Sanford. His father left the family when he was four. Redd's mother moved with him to Chicago, when he was thirteen; then she abandoned him. At that point, his grandmother took over raising the young teen. While living in Chicago, he and three friends formed a band called the Bon-Bons. The trio moved to New York City three years later and eventually disbanded. Foxx began doing stand-up comedy in small clubs around the country. It was at this point he began using the name that would stick with him for the rest of his life. He chose Redd, a nickname he earned due to his reddish hair and complexion, along with Foxx, which he took from baseball star Jimmie Foxx.

Early in life, he brushed shoulders with Harold Washington, the future mayor of Chicago, and Malcolm Little, who later became Malcolm X. In fact, in his biography, Malcolm X refers to Foxx as "Chicago Red, the funniest dishwasher on this earth."

Foxx played before both black and white audiences, and made numerous appearances on national television talk shows, including *The Today Show*, *Merv Griffin*, and *The Tonight Show*. There's no doubt that Redd influenced many of today's black comics, including Chris Rock, Bernie Mac, and Eddie Murphy.

Foxx was very loyal to his friends. Beginning in 1951 and running through 1955, he and comedian Slappy White worked the small clubs together, doing a routine that was very adult oriented. In fact, they became known as Redd, White, and Blue. Later on, White would be a part of Foxx's television shows *Sanford and Son* and *The Redd Foxx Comedy Hour*.

Foxx recorded numerous comedy albums, most of which were considered "blue" at the time. Ossie Davis used Foxx in his 1972 film *Cotton Comes to Harlem,* where he was seen by Norman Lear. The producer promptly signed Foxx as junk dealer Fred Sanford in the NBC sitcom *Sanford and Son.* The show was a huge hit, running for eleven seasons. After the show became so popular and the actor became a household name, Foxx ran into problems with NBC. After his popularity soared, he was unable to renegotiate his contract with NBC, even to the point where Foxx left the show for a few episodes because he said NBC wouldn't give him a dressing room with a window. He was forced to return to finish out the run of the show after the company put out an injunction which didn't allow him to work for any other network while he was still under his contract with them.

After his contract was up with NBC, ABC made him a lucrative offer and he jumped ship, establishing *The Redd Foxx Comedy Hour* on his new television home. The variety show had a very loose structure, and with Redd as executive producer, he took a new approach with the program. One of his most popular portions of the show was when he took live questions from the audience, answering them with his usual wit and charm.

After the *The Redd Foxx Comedy Hour* was cancelled, Foxx took Las Vegas by storm, becoming an instant headliner in Sin

City. In fact, he was the first black comedian to perform to white audiences on the Las Vegas strip. He had performed there early in his career at the Sahara Lounge and was a popular entertainer even before the television shows made him a household name across America.

In 1968, the International Hotel offered the comic $960 thousand dollars to do a 32-week run in its showroom. Foxx agreed and sold out every show in the series. Other Las Vegas casinos where he performed included the Castaways and the Aladdin. When at the Silverbird, he taped an HBO special which is available on DVD.

In 1989, Foxx co-starred with friend Della Reese in Eddie Murphy's *Harlem Nights*, which led to CBS signing the two of them to a new sitcom, *The Royal Family*. It was while filming this sitcom that Foxx had a heart attack and died while on the set of the show, on October 11, 1991.

Like many entertainers who go from making next to nothing to millions of dollars a year, the comedian had been easy with his money and generous to his friends. Once he moved to Las Vegas, he became a gambler, albeit not a good one. Unfortunately, he lost most of his savings, at which time he pulled enough funds together to build his home at Eastern Avenue and Rawhide Street. Not surprisingly, Foxx was also not a great businessman, and the IRS discovered that he owed them a great deal of money. They seized his assets, including his beloved home, and auctioned them in 1989 in order to collect the money he owed them. Fox was later quoted by *People* magazine as saying that the agents didn't even treat him like he was a human being.

After the IRS took the house, Foxx vowed that when he died, he wouldn't go to heaven or hell, but would return to Las Vegas and live in his confiscated home. Apparently, Foxx was a man of his word. Redd's house has been called the most haunted house in Las Vegas. Eight different businesses have bought the house, only to sell it after reporting "strange" happenings on the premises.

After he died, an Elvis impersonator bought the house and lived there with his uncle, both of whom confirmed that the place was haunted. They said the lights would come on at night, doors would open, glasses would break, and the closet door in Redd's room would slam shut. They claimed that the sliding glass door in the back of the house would open and close by itself, and the floors creaked at night like somebody was walking, even when

no one was there. Nine months later, the house was back on the market. It has been bought and sold by other commercial enterprises whose owners and employees all claimed it to be haunted. Foxx was proud of the home, the only house he ever owned, and seems determined to stay there.

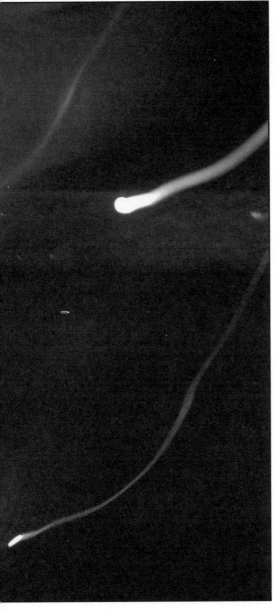

A group of real estate agents who bought the building finally said *enough is enough* and they brought in a group of exorcists to see what Foxx wanted. The exorcists told them that the comedian wanted them to paint a red fox on the side of their sign in front of the business, so when people saw it they would know it was his home. The owners agreed to do so, and also put up lights to further distinguish the house.

The owner has gone so far as to play old recordings by the comedian in order to make friends with him. Things have improved, but Foxx still stops by to visit. Coffee cups often disappear, coffee gets spilled for no reason, and filing cabinet drawers fly open. Redd appears to

Orb in front of realty sign at Redd Foxx's former home.
Photo by Liz Cavanaugh.

still not be happy that the IRS took his house and someone else now occupies it, so he continues to visit the premises, scaring unsuspecting employees and visitors.

After Redd died, the IRS confiscated even more of his assets. His wife didn't have money to properly bury him, so Eddie Murphy paid for the funeral, which was attended by 600 people, including numerous stars from Hollywood and Las Vegas, as well as a host of friends.

There's even an ironic twist to the last episode with the IRS. Robert Allan, who runs Haunted Vegas Tours, says that, when the IRS came, they took just about everything Redd owned except a dilapidated old truck, a red 1951 Ford, that sat in the driveway. They thought it was junk and they didn't want it. The agents neglected to notice the sign on the side of the vehicle that said "Sanford & Son Salvage Yard." It was the truck he drove while making the television sitcom for eleven years. His fourth widow, Korean-born Kaho Cho, sold the truck for $50,000 dollars!

Foxx is buried with his mother, Mary Carson, in Palm Memorial Park in Las Vegas, in the Devotion Section, Lawn Space 4091, 311 G. The grave is located on the left and towards the middle of the section inside the main entrance of the cemetery.

13

BINION MURDER: A LITTLE WEIRD EVEN FOR LAS VEGAS

When Ted Binion was found dead in his home in Las Vegas on September 17, 1998, indications were that the casino executive had died of an overdose. Sandy Murphy, Binion's girlfriend, was the person who called 911 and reported that Binion wasn't breathing. When paramedics entered the house, they found Binion lying on a mattress with no pulse. They thought he had probably been dead for several hours. Police found empty pill bottles near the body, and Xanax, heroin, and traces of Valium were found in the body during the autopsy.

It was commonly known that Binion was a drug user, so at first, there was no suspicion that the death might have been anything other than an overdose. In fact, Binion had purchased twelve pieces of tar heroin and had filled a prescription for Xanax the day before his death. Investigators thought the death to be an overdose or possibly suicide. Murphy later told police that Binion had been suicidal since he lost his gaming license earlier that year. His sister, Barbara, was also a drug addict and had committed suicide in 1977. The death was ruled an overdose, despite the fact that investigators were suspicious that the scene at Binion's house might have been staged. They thought that his body didn't show the typical signs of a drug overdose, plus there was heroin in his stomach, which aroused suspicion since it wasn't thought that a person would take heroin in a way that would result in it being in the stomach.

The death of Binion took on a new twist when Rick Tabish, who was found to be Murphy's lover, was caught a couple of days later at the location of Binion's fortune that was buried in the desert outside of Las Vegas. When he was caught, his friend, Michael Milot, was with him at a vault that concealed the treasure. Tabish told the jury at his murder trial that Binion asked him to dig up the silver in the desert and secure it for his daughter if anything ever happened to him.

Ted's younger sister, Becky, told police she thought her brother had not committed suicide but had been murdered. Police also found out that Binion knew Murphy, a former stripper, was cheating on him and that he had removed her from his will the day before he died.

Binion, who was fifty-four at the time of his death, was the son of Las Vegas casino owner Lester Ben "Benny" Binion of Binion's Horseshoe fame. Ted and his brother, Jack, held the gaming license to the casino after their father was charged with tax evasion and other offenses. Ted's title was casino manager, and he soon became well known as the host of the casino's poker tournaments. His life was what one might expect of a man in his position – parties, celebrity guests, and women seeking his attention. There was another side to Binion, too, that of a man who loved to read and was interested in history, especially that surrounding the Civil War. He was also a math genius and was quick to help those who needed financial aid.

Binion's life was not without problems. He had been the target of a kidnapping earlier in his life, and he was a known heroin and marijuana user. He was arrested in 1986 on drug trafficking charges, which drew attention to his connection to "Fat Herbie" Blitzstein, an organized crime figure well known to police. At the time, officials suspected that Binion was using Murphy as his bagwoman. By 1996, he was banned from running or being on the premises of the Horseshoe Casino. In 1998, his license was permanently revoked and he was unable to participate in the casino business again.

At that time, Binion was forced to move his collection of silver from the vault at the Horseshoe Casino. Ted decided to stash it in the desert in a twelve-foot vault on land he owned near Pahrump, about sixty miles west of Las Vegas. When police found Tabish at the vault a couple days after Binion's death, they discovered six tons of silver bullion, Horseshoe Casino chips, paper currency, and more than 100,000 rare coins, including Carson City silver dollars, many in mint condition. Total worth of the stash was estimated to be between $7 million and $14 million. Interestingly, when Binion decided to built the vault, he asked his friend Rick Tabish to construct it. He then transferred his valuables to the vault, using MRT Transport, a trucking company owned by Tabish. Police found out that the only two people who had the combination to the storage vault were Binion and Tabish. Tabish later said he asked Binion if he wanted to change the combination so that only he would know it but Ted declined to do so.

Six months after Binion's death had been ruled an overdose, in May of 1999, the coroner's office declared it a homicide, and a full-scale investigation began. A month later, Murphy and Tabish were arrested for Binion's murder and were charged with conspiracy, robbery, grand larceny, and burglary. The case was built around the idea that the two lovers conspired to kill Binion and steal the valuables he had in his vault in the desert. An expert witness, Dr. Michael Baden, told the jury that he thought Binion had been killed by two people by a method called "burking," a form of asphyxiation. He also said that because Binion was known to inhale the heroin vapors instead of snorting them, it was very unlikely that he had died of a drug overdose. He said there were not enough drugs in Binion's body to cause an overdose. A jury took eight days to convict Murphy and Tabish. Each was initially found guilty of murder, with Tabish getting a sentence of twenty-five years to life and Murphy receiving twenty-two years to life.

The defendants appealed the decision, and in July of 2003, the Nevada Supreme Court overturned the murder convictions. The reason for the decision was that Clark County District Court Judge Joseph Bonaventure had made a mistake when he was instructing the jury on their deliberations. It seems that the court thought that the jury could have been prejudiced against Tabish, who was also charged with assault and blackmail of another businessman. These charges were brought up in the trial despite the fact that they were never directly linked to the Binion murder. Additionally, the court ruled that the jurors should have been told that an attorney for Binion's estate made statements that should have been considered opinion, not fact.

A new trial began on October 11, 2004, again in Judge Bonaventure's courtroom. Murphy and Tabish each faced six counts of murder and/or robbery, murder in the first or second degree, and robbery. They were found not guilty of conspiracy to commit murder and/or robbery, murder in the first or second degree, and robbery. The lovers were found guilty of conspiracy to commit burglary and/or larceny, burglary, and grand larceny. The jury, which deliberated for seventeen hours, did not find the two guilty of murder because they said there was not enough forensic evidence to prove them guilty without reasonable doubt. Murphy did not have to go back to prison on her conviction because of the time she had already served. Tabish was returned to prison with the possibility of parole in 2009.

The trial was filled with what many called suspect testimony. Kurt Gratzer testified that he and Tabish had discussed ways to kill Binion. Deanna Perry, who worked as a manicurist, said Murphy predicted Binion would overdose a week before the actual incident. She also said Murphy said her "new, rich boyfriend" would get Binion's silver. It was later discovered that the defense had paid Gratzer $20,000 to take care of outstanding bills.

In talking to members of the jury after the second trial, newspaper reports said that they didn't buy the prosecution theory that Binion had been suffocated by Tabish and Murphy because medical testimony didn't support that. The jurors were more inclined to think of the death as an accidental overdose because of Binion's previous drug use and because of testimony by defense experts who said that heroin and Xanax were the cause of death, despite the fact that there were no fingerprints on the Xanax bottle. Prosecutors said this was an indication that the scene had been wiped down after the alleged murder. It was felt that, because police initially thought the death an overdose, they may not have taken proper precautions to secure evidence at the scene.

Gratzer told the first jury that Tabish tried to hire him to kill Binion less than a month before he was found dead. He said Tabish offered to pay him a portion of a life insurance policy that Murphy would collect. He also said it was Tabish's idea to use Xanax because it would make the death look like a suicide. Gratzer later contradicted much of the information he gave to police about Tabish. He said he had told them Murphy had nothing to do with the murder. He said he had told them that Tabish told him that Murphy knew nothing about the plot to murder Binion. He also said he was one of seven people who received reward money from the Binion estate. Gratzer did mention that Murphy was not connected to the murder early in his testimony to police because the *Las Vegas Mercury* wrote about it early on in its coverage of the murder and subsequent trial.

The high profile case was the subject of several television shows and books. The television series "CSI" used it as a basis for its September 27, 2002 episode, entitled "Burked." Several books, *Death in the Desert* by Cathy Scott, *Murder in Sin City* by Jeff German, and *Positively Fifth Street* by James McManus, were published about the case. In 2008, a made-for-TV movie, *Sex & Lies in Sin City*, based on German's book, aired. Mena Suvari and Matthew Modine starred in the original movie for the Lifetime Network.

14

BOBBY HATFIELD CAN'T LET GO OF HIS FAVORITE PLACE IN LAS VEGAS

When Bobby Hatfield and Bill Medley formed the Righteous Brothers in 1962, their dream was to put together a duo that would be good enough to play in Las Vegas. In 1964, the pair were working the lounge at the Sands Hotel, performing three shows a night, solidifying their act, and learning to entertain the crowd. Ironically, the pair found a home in Vegas at the Orleans Showroom late in their career, a room where Bobby loved to perform. Apparently, Hatfield loves Las Vegas so much that he continues to honor it with his presence.

As a duo, Bobby and Bill made musical history with many chart records, including their mega hit "You've Lost That Loving Feeling." The performance rights organization, Broadcast Music Inc. (BMI), has logged more than eight million airplays for the tune which was released in 1965. The men didn't expect the song to be a hit, as it was longer than most music out at that time and a ballad, plus it was being released at the height of the invasion of British groups to the American music scene.

Although Medley and Hatfield called it quits as a duo in 1968, they continued to perform as solo acts. The two joined forces again in 1974, pulling in a top ten pop hit with their recording of "Rock And Roll Heaven." They continued to perform as a duo and as solo performers, even staging a twenty-year reunion tour in 1982.

Several of the duo's songs, including "You've Lost That Loving Feeling," showed up in movies like *Top Gun*. It was in 1990, though, that the pair had their biggest comeback. The movie *Ghost*, starring Patrick Swayze and Demi Moore, featured their hit "Unchained Melody" in one of the major love scenes in the movie. Bill and Bobby found themselves thrust back into the limelight. The duo immediately re-recorded the tune and released it in 1991, twenty-five years after the song first was a hit. The song quickly achieved Platinum status with sales of over a million. The new recording also garnered them a Grammy nod for Best Pop Performance for a Duo or Group with Vocal. "Unchained Melody" has been called the best love song of all time.

The singers met while performing solo gigs in Orange County, California. One night, they sang together and, after hearing the reaction of the audience, they decided they might be stronger together than apart. Their decision proved right as they had hit after hit in addition to the ones mentioned above, including "Ebb Tide" and "You're My Soul and Inspiration." As the story goes, the name The Righteous Brothers came about when a Marine called out after one of their duets, "That's righteous, brothers." A deejay in Philadelphia conjured up the term "blue-eyed soul" to describe the duo, coined because they were white singers performing with the soul of the black performers of the time. The duo won numerous awards over the years, including induction into the Rock and Roll Hall of Fame in March of 2003. At the time, they were still touring. Just eight months later, Bobby Hatfield was dead.

The guys were just starting a tour and were booked to play a gig at Western Michigan University's Miller Auditorium in Kalamazoo on November 5th, 2003. The duo had performed in New Orleans for the last time just prior to heading out to Michigan. When Hatfield didn't show up at call time, someone was sent to the hotel to find him. Half an hour before they were to go on, the singer was found dead in his hotel room. There were 2,400 people waiting at Miller Auditorium to see the Righteous Brothers on the opening night of a four-day swing through Michigan and Ohio. The fans were told the show was being cancelled

due to a "personal emergency of an unspecified nature." Soon, the news of Hatfield's death was released, with the cause given being a heart attack. A few days later, the medical examiner announced that post-mortem toxicology results indicated that Hatfield's heart attack was caused by acute cocaine intoxication, not by advanced coronary disease. The report was amended to reflect those results.

Hatfield, who was sixty-three, is buried at Pacific View Memorial Park, Corona del Mar, Orange County, California. Yet it is in Las Vegas where reports of Bobby's ghost have been seen.

The Righteous Brothers performed in Las Vegas four or five times a year, even calling it their favorite place to play. After Hatfield's death, Bill Medley returned to the city to do a tribute to his late partner. As the show ended, the whole band came to the front of the stage to take their bows. There was a loud pop, and everyone started to look around to see what was going on. They immediately saw glass shards all over one part of the stage. When they looked up they saw that one of the Par Cans had exploded through the gel, actually melting the gel that covered it. It took them only a minute to realize that the Par Can was the one that normally would have been over Bobby's head. That was only the first of numerous other appearances by what many folks consider to be Hatfield's spirit.

One of the people who worked with the Righteous Brothers recalls numerous

Mist in hallway believed to be frequented by Bobby Hatfield's spirit. *Photo by Liz Cavanaugh.*

instances of feeling Bobby's presence around them. "I would feel someone walk by and brush my hair. When I turned around, there wouldn't be anyone there."

There are also stories about a cleaning lady who has seen Hatfield as well. The lady says she sees someone walking down the hallway near the stage wearing a patterned shirt. Hatfield usually wore colorful shirts very much like the ones the cleaning lady describes seeing on the ghostly apparition. Someone who worked with the duo recalled that Bobby was quite the prankster and was always pulling jokes on them when the pair played the showroom.

One day proved particularly intriguing for some of the people who had worked with Bobby and Bill. Interestingly enough, it started with a person who does not really believe in the ghosts of the dead returning to visit this earth. He remembers feeling someone walk past him. The light person also was having trouble with their board that same day. When the two people mentioned it, somebody jokingly said it was probably Bobby up to his old tricks of playing pranks on them. It really made them think when someone finally remembered that it was Bobby's birthday that day.

Other people recall walking along the catwalk in the club and feeling someone go past them. Still other folks remember feeling someone walk past them and grab their hair or touch them, but when they turn around no one is there. Sometimes the toilet will flush in what had been the Righteous Brothers dressing room, but no one will be in the area.

Folks who worked with Hatfield think he's just continuing to amuse them with his bag of tricks. "There's nothing to be afraid of," one of the people who knew him says. "But the lady who does the cleaning does get a little freaked out because she's usually working by herself when she sees him, and she says she sees him all the time."

"It really wouldn't surprise me at all if it is him we sense at different times because he loved performing in Las Vegas," another worker says. "I think it's a real possibility that he does come back here to visit."

While there is no record of anyone outside the folks who knew him seeing Bobby, his spirit continues to visit the city that he loved most to play—Las Vegas, Nevada.

15

THE DEATH
OF TUPAC SHAKUR

Tupac Shakur hit the trifecta when it came to talent; he was a successful rapper, a successful actor, and a well-known social activist. He was one of the best selling hip-hop artists of all time, selling more than 75 million records worldwide. His songs tell stories of life in the ghetto, racism, hardship, and violence, lots of violence.

Getting his start as a roadie and backup dancer for the group Digital Underground, the Brooklyn, New York, native was living the dream when his debut album, *2Pacalypse Now*, received both criticism and critical acclaim. Throughout his short life, Shakur became the target of several lawsuits and various legal problems.

He was shot and robbed in the lobby of a New York recording studio in 1994. The ordeal made Tupac uneasy, and he began to take a second look at the other rappers he associated with and the men who made the decisions in the hip-hop world. He felt that people around him might have been aware that the shooting was going to take place, but didn't bother to clue him in. His suspicions and the controversy surrounding them added fuel to the rivalry between East Coast and West Coast hip-hop adversaries.

After serving an eleven-month sentence for sexual abuse, Shakur was released from prison. Suge Knight, CEO of Death

Row Records, financed his appeal. In exchange for his assistance, Tupac signed a three -album deal with Suge and the label.

On Saturday, September 7th, 1996, Mike Tyson and Bruce Seldon's boxing match at the MGM Grand was the hottest ticket in town. The guest list included a who's who of Hollywood stars, Wall Street high rollers, music moguls, drug lords, and a few mobsters mixed in for good measure. Tupac Shakur and Death Row Record's Suge Knight also attended the fight.

Less than two minutes after it got underway, the boxing match was over when Tyson knocked out Seldon. Around 8:45, Shakur and other members of the Death Row entourage, which reportedly included several bodyguards and other people from the record company, got into an argument with a young black man while leaving the event. The quarrel escalated into a fight, which was captured on the MGM Grand's security cameras. The hotel's security team quickly broke up the altercation, and Tupac, Suge, and their entourage left the property.

Tupac and his group headed to the Luxor, where Tupac was reported to be staying. They were only at the Luxor a few minutes before heading to Knight's home in Southeast Las Vegas. Both men changed clothes and headed to an appearance at an anti-gang event, which was being held at a nightclub called Club 662, owned by Knight, on East Flamingo Road. The club's name was supposedly symbolic of how gangs had infiltrated the rap business. On a phone keypad, 662 spells "mob."

Around 11:15pm, Tupac and Knight, riding in Knight's Black BMW 750, turned off Las Vegas Boulevard and headed down Flamingo Road. Knight was driving with Tupac in the passenger seat. Tupac was happy and seemingly enjoying himself as he waved to fans on the street. Oblivious to any danger, they didn't see the white Cadillac that was following them.

While stopped at a traffic light in front of the Maxim Hotel, the white Caddy pulled up to the light. There were four people inside. In a flash, one of the passengers took out a high caliber Glock and fired several shots into Knight's car. Tupac was shot at least four times; Knight suffered a minor wound to his head.

The white Cadillac sped away. Some witnesses claimed that Suge Knight returned fire, but that remains unclear.

Tupac was in bad shape. Knight pulled away, but was stopped blocks away by Las Vegas Police, who called for medical assistance. Tupac was rushed to University Medical Center. He was immediately taken to the first of two surgeries that were performed that night. Family and friends began a vigil of prayer that lasted until Friday, September 13th, when, at 4:03pm, Tupac Amaru Shakur died of respiratory failure and cardiopulmonary arrest.

Ironically, Shakur, who always wore a bulletproof vest, wasn't wearing it that night. He was just twenty-five-years-old. Three days before the shootings, Tupac was in New York for the MTV Video Music Awards, where he surrounded himself with bodyguards and kept a walkie-talkie in his hand. Insiders suspected that Tupac knew at the time that something was brewing, but no one talked.

His family had his body cremated and held a private memorial service the next day. In the days that followed, twelve people, who are reported to have either been involved or were holding information related to Tupac's shooting, were killed or wounded in a series of separate shootings.

There are many theories about who killed Tupac. Most center around the thirty-year rivalry between the retaliating Bloods and Crips and Tupac's ties with the Bloods. Some say it was set up by Suge Knight himself. Odds are good that the truth will never come out. The killing of the world's most famous rap star remains officially unsolved. Las Vegas police have never made an arrest.

The Maxim Hotel and Casino no longer exist. The property which originally opened in 1977, closed in 1999. Though smaller than typical Vegas resorts even before today's mega-resort era, the Maxim had a popular following because of its attention to personal service. Its glory days were in the 1980s.

Today, the Westin Casuarinas Las Vegas Hotel, Casino & Spa stands where the Maxim once held court. Located at 160 East Flamingo Road, the hotel is a beautiful property that claims to be a sanctuary amidst the bustle of the Las Vegas Strip, a place to retreat whenever you need some peace.

Across the street is an unassuming lamp post covered with writing and graffiti. The post has become a memorial to the late rapper, marking the spot where he was shot. The chain link fence behind it often sports condolence notes and memorials, along with flowers, candles, and small stuffed animals. Every five or six weeks the city has to repaint the post to cover the writings. Tupac's devoted fans still gather at the site to pay homage to their fallen star. On more than one occasion, people reportedly have seen the ghostly image of a man resembling Tupac walking around the post area as if he were lost.

More often than not, Tupac's ghost is supposedly seen roaming his Las Vegas mansion, pacing back and forth across the front balcony of his house. The devoted and the curious still drive by the house at all hours of the night taking photos of the mansion and upsetting the high brow neighbors.

The house sits on a private upscale street, difficult to spot unless you know exactly where you're looking. These days the street lights are turned off at night so as not to draw attention to the elaborate mansions along the street and to maintain the privacy of the people who own them. Although Tupac sometimes lived in the house, it was actually owned by Suge Knight.

The estate reportedly boasts four bedrooms, six bathrooms, and a personal spa. It is located in the Sierra Vista Rancho Estates on Monte Rosa Avenue. It has recently been sold, but not before it fell into disrepair. Knight, some people say, had the swimming pool painted blood red. The deck also was red, as was the master-bedroom carpet. It is believed Knight did this in honor of the Bloods; the gang that originated in his hometown of Compton, California.

16

THE EL RANCHO AND THE THUNDERBIRD

It would be impossible to talk about Las Vegas hotels without mentioning the El Rancho. Built in 1941, The El Rancho sat at the corner of Highway 91 South, directly across from where the Sahara is today. It had 110 rooms and was, at that time, the largest hotel in Las Vegas. Today, that little ribbon of Highway is known as the Las Vegas Strip. The El Rancho was the template from which all the modern resort casinos were grown.

Conceived by Thomas Hull, the El Rancho was the first "destination" resort where a guest could have a fine meal, enjoy all kinds of entertainment, sleep in a nice room, and gamble. In the early days of Vegas, you would have had to go to a restaurant for dining, a gambling hall to try your luck, a motel to sleep, and a nightclub to see the performers. The concept was an instant hit. Within a year of the opening, other hotels with casinos began popping up on Highway 91 South, and soon a new era of gaming was established. Visitors to the desert city now had a choice between spending their money at the exciting new upscale Strip resorts and the less cultured and seedy options around Fremont Street.

Although the El Rancho never achieved the status of some of her successors, such as the Tropicana, she was a well respected property with a profitable casino and hotel. Hull had built the property as part of his "El Rancho" chain which included similar resort type properties in Bakersfield and Sacramento. Hull didn't retain ownership of the property for long, and it soon began changing hands on a frequent basis. One owner, Beldon Katleman, began bringing in name acts to lure high spenders to the showroom and ultimately to the casino. He is also credited with creating "revue" style shows that are still popular in Las Vegas today.

In 1960, a fire swept through the hotel. Although no one was seriously injured, the hotel was completely destroyed. The cause of the fire was officially listed as arson, but no one was ever arrested for the crime. Ironically, the property's fire insurance was paid up. Management said that over $500 thousand in cash had burned in the fire. Harry James and Betty Grable were headlining in the Opera House showroom when the fire broke out, but they managed to escape unscathed.

The hotel was never rebuilt. Howard Hughes's Hughes Corporation bought the casino and tried to keep it running as a stand-alone gaming hall as long as they could. Eventually, they closed the doors and the property became a storage facility before that building finally was leveled into a parking lot. Hilton Hotels eventually bought part of the property and built their Hilton Timeshare project on a section of it. In 2007, the MGM Mirage Corporation, in partnership with Kerzner International, purchased the remaining acres and announced plans to build a new resort casino on the site.

In 1982, the Thunderbird Hotel and Casino was renovated and renamed the El Rancho. The original Thunderbird Hotel opened in 1948. Faced with mounting financial obligations and no longer able to compete with the multimillion dollar behemoths on the Strip, like so many other legendary hotels, it closed in 1992.

Named after a Navajo tribal legend, the Thunderbird had a Native American theme, complete with the "Pow Wow Showroom" and a neon eagle on top of their famous sign. Despite losing nearly $145 thousand to lucky craps players on its first night of business, the 76-room property soon became so popular, another 170 guest rooms were added. By 1953, the popularity of the hotel continued to outweigh room availability and a 110-room motel and bar-restaurant called the Algiers was added. As with most other popular hotels and casinos in Vegas, the Thunderbird attracted its share of unwanted attention. In the mid fifties, it became a focal point of a congressional investigation into organized crime. The hotel remained open, as did its casino, but the outcome of the investigation led gaming officials to keep a closer eye on casino operations and ultimately led to the formation of the Nevada State Gaming Control Board.

While there are no known stories of ghosts associated with the original El Rancho or the Thunderbird, there is an interesting story that surfaced shortly after the implosion of the main building. According to local rumors, the building is being haunted by ghosts. KVBC News 3 of Las Vegas did an investigation into the haunting and discovered that most of the structure was rotten; still, a handful of operating slot machines and some totally renovated and maintained rooms remained. Why did the rooms survive and the slots continue to work? Who were the guests that remained to use them?

Today, The Turnberry Place condominium complex stands on the site of the Thunderbird Hotel and Casino, although the land is slated to be the site for the new Fontainebleau Resort.

The Thunderbird Hotel and Casino might be most remembered as the hotel that helped establish Las Vegas as a center for conventions and trade shows. It will also fondly be remembered as the place where singer Rosemary Clooney made her first appearance in Las Vegas in 1951, and where Judy Garland, who would die of a drug overdose four years later, made her final appearance in 1965.

17

WHISKEY PETE'S HOTEL AND CASINO

They say that guests at Whiskey Pete's Hotel and Casino often arrive with their gas tanks low only to mysteriously find the tank full when they return to their vehicle. With gas prices at record highs, it might be a good time to route yourself through the small town of Primm and pay a visit to Whiskey Pete's.

Whiskey Pete's is located at 100 W. Primm Boulevard, in Primm, Nevada, roughly forty miles southwest of the Las Vegas Strip, near the California/Nevada border. The property is a familiar stop for Californians desperate to toss a few last coins in slots before returning home. It's a cheery Western-themed place that replicates an early 1800s mining town. The compound is family friendly (the pool even has a waterslide), pet friendly (good for poker playing dogs), and very reasonably priced. Your host is a big welcoming cartoon mascot with an oversized moustache (supposedly Whiskey Pete himself) holding a bag of money and a jug of moonshine. With over 700 newly renovated guestrooms and suites and lots of great places to rustle up a meal, Whiskey Pete's (nicknamed "The Castle of the Desert") has come a long, long way from its humble beginnings as a two-pump gas station in the middle of nowhere.

So who was Whiskey Pete? He was a cranky old codger whose real name was Pete McIntyre. Pete had a little gas station that sat on the site where the hotel and casino are today. Apparently, the gas business wasn't enough to support his favorite pastime of drinking, so Pete began making a little moonshine and eventually built up a nice little bootlegging business. As the legend goes, Pete died in 1933. It was his wish to be buried standing up with a bottle of moonshine in his hand, wearing his trademark cowboy hat and boots. McIntyre felt this would enable him to watch over his property a bit easier after his demise. Sadly, many years later, his strangely angled coffin was accidentally dug up during some construction work on the hotel. Supposedly, Pete McIntyre was reburied in one of the caves where he brewed his moonshine, but no real proof of this can be found.

Guests have reported seeing a ghostly image ambling around the casino from time to time; other hotels guests have reported lights going on and off in their hotel rooms, and objects mysteriously moving from place to place. Could it be Whiskey Pete? Possibly, but it could also be the ghost of a young boy that went missing from the hotel one day. Seven-year-old Alexander Harris from Mountain View, California, disappeared from the hotel's video arcade in November of 1987. The boy was on a trip with his parents, who were in the casino at the time of his abduction. A massive search was conducted for the boy with no results. Tragically, a little over a month later, his lifeless body was discovered beneath a trailer allegedly belonging to the hotel's manager. The coroners' report concluded that he had been suffocated.

A computer analyst named Howard Lee Haupt was arrested and charged with the kidnapping and boy's murder. In 1989, Haupt was acquitted of the charges. He later was awarded a million dollar settlement after he filed a lawsuit against the Las Vegas Police Department, saying that his civil rights had been violated by the detectives working the case. A federal judge later declared the amount excessive and overturned the decision. After battling for several years, Haupt eventually settled for reimbursement of his legal fees.

No one else has ever been charged with Alexander Harris's murder.

The Las Vegas police still contend that Haupt is the killer, but he can't be retried for the crime.

For several years, the Whiskey Pete's hotel lobby was home to the bullet-ridden car that Bonnie and Clyde died in. Tourists flocked to take photos standing beside the infamous vehicle. It is now on display in another Primm, Nevada, casino.

So is Whiskey Pete really the resident ghost or is it the little boy who never received justice?

18

THE UNION PLAZA HOTEL & CASINO

When the Plaza Hotel opened on July 2, 1971, it was the crowning gem of the downtown area and claimed the same fleeting bragging rights as several other Las Vegas hotels. It was the largest and tallest hotel in all of Las Vegas; at least it was on July 2nd, 1971. However, in a city like Las Vegas, no one holds on to bragging rights very long.

The original name was the Union Plaza Hotel because the Union Pacific railroad station was located on the property. It was the only train station in America connected to a casino. When Amtrak roared through Vegas with its *Desert Wind*, a passenger train route operated from October 1979 to May 1997, the train station's ticket office was connected to the hotel. In 1997, the *Desert Wind's* route was discontinued due to budget cuts and replaced with Los Angeles-Las Vegas Thruway Motorcoach service. Somewhere along the line, the "Union" was dropped from the name and the property simple became The Plaza Hotel & Casino.

Although the hotel's restaurants and casino have been used for many major Hollywood films and videos, the hotel's popularity has dwindled over the past few years. If you catch a late night James Bond marathon, you can plainly see the hotel under construction in *Diamonds Are Forever*.

Located in Downtown Las Vegas, directly across from Freemont Street, the Plaza Hotel now caters to mainly tourists looking for an inexpensive place to grab a few winks and gamble, although several good restaurants, a swimming pool with individual cabanas, and planned renovations ensure that it remains possibly the best hotel in the Freemont Street area. The showroom of the hotel features a variety of entertainment. Currently, the long running "Rat Pack" plays daily with impersonators paying tribute to Frank and the gang. But for many years those familiar with the showroom have suspected there's more going on there than just a show.

Guests have often said they felt a cold spot in the showroom or had chills that had nothing to do with the performance. It's rumored that a stagehand, who worked there at one time, committed suicide and his ghost has simply refused to leave. Back stage props seem to move around and become misplaced, often confusing and frightening the current crop of stage hands.

A few "long-timers" who work the theatre have another theory. They suspect the spirit of Houdini haunts the showroom. A magic show honoring the legendary performer ran in the showroom for many years and some think Houdini might have been hanging around to make sure the show was done right. A few of the hotel's guests have reported cold spots on the escalators and dark hallways in the oldest parts of the hotel and other say they have a feeling that someone is always watching you, and they don't mean security cameras.

While the Plaza still plays host to corporate meetings and events, it's better known for its reasonably priced wedding receptions and Quinceaneras. There is also a Sunday Celebrity Brunch hosted by Magnum PI's Larry Manetti, as well as the always popular $7.77 buffet. The hotel is still a decent value for the money with a lot of dining options and an 80,000 square foot casino. For those longing to relive the seventies, downtown Las Vegas is still the place to go.

These days, a slow economy and inability to compete with the hotels on the Strip isn't the only problem facing the Plaza.

Its biggest problem is its name. While located in the downtown area for more than thirty years, the Las Vegas Plaza Hotel is not the household name that the world-renowned, and very posh, Plaza Hotel in New York City is. So, guess what famous New York Hotel is building a replica on the Las Vegas Strip?

Business leaders claim there's room for two Plaza hotels in Las Vegas. Tamares Las Vegas Properties, owners of the downtown Plaza, sought to block Elad Group (representing the New York Plaza) from using the Plaza name because Tamares officials think the presence of two Plazas will create confusion in the market. Time will tell, but for now it looks like there will be two vastly different Plaza Hotels to accommodate potential guests of all incomes in Sin City.

19

THE TROPICANA AND KALANAU

On the corner of Las Vegas Boulevard and Tropicana Avenue sits the world-famous Tropicana Hotel. A foot bridge high above the traffic links the hotel to The Excalibur to the west and the MGM Grand to the north. Built in 1957, the hotel's celebrated grand opening took place on April 4 of that year. It marked the beginning of a new era of high-end resorts and was, without a doubt, the finest first-class resort facility in all of Nevada.

Nicknamed the "Tiffany of the Strip" by the *Saturday Evening Post*, the Tropicana was the epitome of undisputed elegance and sophistication.

Opening night in the posh hotel's lavish showroom, then called the Theatre Restaurant, was filled to capacity as headliner Eddie Fisher entertained the elite. In 1959, the hotel brought the world-renowned Folies Begere to the main showroom where it still plays today. The hotel was originally designed as a destination resort for the affluent; however, like most of the hotels in Las Vegas, it soon added a casino to bring in additional revenue.

The hotel was surrounded by lavish grounds and colorful tropical gardens around an Olympic-sized pool, tennis courts and, eventually, an eighteen-hole championship golf course. The buildings were situated in a "Y" shape that enabled guests to be served in a fast and efficient manner made even easier by a staff-to-guest ratio of one to one. The original hotel consisted of 300 rooms located in the Garden Tower, while the Paradise and Tiffany Towers were added in 1979.

The Tropicana continued to expand and evolve. By 1984, the resort spread over thirty-six acres and offered something for everyone. From five-star restaurants and boutique shops to a high-tech sports complex, the Tropicana worked hard to maintain its cutting edge. A five-acre water park and another twenty-two-story addition, The Island Tower, were added in 1986.

So, now that you know the basics, are there any ghosts lurking around the Tropicana? None that anyone has reported; however, The Tropicana had something better.

As the hotel continued to evolve and change to keep up with the times, a 1991 renovation introduced the Tropicana's Outer Island, which included two thirty-five-foot Aku Aku gods. Each Aku Aku god weighed in at a hefty 300,000 pounds, making them quite unpopular with would-be souvenir seekers. The best part of the new addition was, without a doubt, the giant tiki mask named Kalanau, which roughly translates to the "God of Money." What better way to greet guests at the entrance of a casino than an enormous "God of Money" that you could virtually reach out and touch! And touching it was exactly what the tourists and good luck hunters did.

Here's where the haunted part comes in. It seems that if you touched the mask, you might end up with a funky purplish-colored rash. Several people reported getting the rash to the hotel's management, but how could you possibly prove that you developed the rash from touching a large decorative mask? Others reported snapping pictures of the giant tiki only to get home, have the shots developed, and find a strange purple haze or fog covering their photos.

The once-grand hotel has since undergone many changes and is still a great resort property; however, the clientele has changed with the times, and the Tropicana now attracts a more budget-conscious family tourist crowd.

Sadly, the famous Kalanau tiki mask is now gone. The unofficial report from the hotel's management is that it was removed because it constantly caused a commotion at the front of the casino with people trying to grab a little luck and a photo. Did all the flashbulbs and rubbing finally get to be too much for Kalanau? Was he angry or just plain tired? Did management try rubbing the mask only to find an itchy purple patch popping up on their palm? We'll never know.

20

THE MGM GRAND GOES UP IN SMOKE

November 21, 1980, was without a doubt the most tragic day in Vegas' history. That was the date when the second most deadly fire in America swept through Kirk Kerkorian's MGM Grand hotel and casino. (The most deadly was when 119 people perished in a December 1946 fire at an Atlanta, Georgia, hotel.)

Though Vegas' firefighters worked valiantly after arriving just four minutes after the alarm at the MGM Grand, eighty-four people died immediately, with two more losing their fight for life months later. Over 500 more were injured, either from the fire itself or from inhalation of the smoke or toxic fumes from the fire.

The fire and its heat were so intense that the hotel's front doors were blown out and even the cars outside the entrance were completely destroyed. Reporter David Spanier said in his *Welcome to the Pleasuredome* that the smoke outside had risen in a nearly mile-high column, that the casino's crystal chandeliers and ceiling panels had crashed down, and that a wall of fire had roared through the building.

Investigation showed that the initial spark was started by an electrical ground fault in the wiring that sent power to a compressor under a pie display case in The Deli at the MGM Grand. It caused smoke to spread rapidly through the building's air conditioning

The employment center of Bally's Hotel and Casino, original site of the kitchen at the MGM Grand where the fire began. *Photo by Liz Cavanaugh.*

system, while the fire raced through the casino and hotel at a rate of nineteen feet per second. Ninety-nine percent of its 2,100 hotel rooms (the largest hotel in the world at that time) were occupied that day, and the casino was full of gamblers, many of whom incredibly kept on gambling even as the fire was beginning to spread.

About 5,000 people were actually in the hotel and casino at the time of the fire, though it was feared at the time that the number was much higher. The property had five restaurants, and it even had its own shopping mall, so it was very fortunate that many of the guests were apparently out of the building then.

Families of the victims received a total of millions of dollars (ranging from $75-$272 million, depending on the source of the report) from Kerkorian, his partners, and their respective insurance companies, but that certainly didn't bring back their loved ones or make the survivors forget their pain and nightmarish memories.

Why were these lives lost? The consensus seems to be greed. Kerkorian and his partners had refused to spend the mere $192 thousand required to install the fire sprinklers in the casino and restaurant that had been recommended by the Local Fire Marshal.

The money was a mere blip on the screen in the MGM Grand's total building cost of $120 million for the twenty-six-story resort hotel, but the owners didn't want any delays in the 1972 opening and the all-important subsequent flow of gambling receipts. The hotel itself did have fire sprinklers, which prevented the actual fire from spreading to the hotel rooms, though it couldn't prevent the smoke from going through the stairwells, elevators, and air-conditioning system. To make it even worse, the alarm system was destroyed by the fire.

Unbelievably, thieves even went into the building while it burned to steal jewelry and money from empty hotel rooms. Greed obviously wasn't a quality limited to the owners of the hotel.

The hotel was rebuilt in eight months, and later was sold to Bally's Manufacturing Company, with the name of the hotel and casino changing to Bally's. Kerkorian built a new MGM Grand in a different location about a mile south. Of course, both had sprinkler systems because, as a direct result of the tragedy, Nevada adopted the strictest fire code laws and regulations for any hotels in America.

In a recent interview for this book, Robert Allen of Haunted Vegas Tours, told us, "I spoke with someone who used to work at Bally's—the old MGM Grand—and there was like an overlay of the old hotel and the new hotel. Everybody will deny this, but the people at the front desk would get all kinds of calls, like from a lady who was just hysterical (because) she had dismembered feet just floating in her room and they would always refer back to see if she was in a room that was part of the trajectory of the original fire.

"I stood outside during the fire and saw the smoke. I watched for hours from across the street and there were people jumping and all kinds of weird stuff. It started in the kitchen, a loose wire or something. It started smoldering then went into the air-conditioning system and eventually right into the tower. The tower was smoking. People were on their balconies cause the rooms had filled with smoke, the halls had filled with smoke. They found people in the stairwells overcome with smoke. I don't think that many people actually were burned, except for the people in the casino. The ball of fire went into the casino and they found people with their hands on melted machines and melted coins," Allen said sorrowfully.

With a confidential air, Allen added, "A man I talked to was a dealer, and he said they won't admit it, that they are told not to even discuss it, but they'll be doing a big night, it'll be really crowded, and they'll see like groups of people just sort of floating all over the other people, and they're see-through, and you think you're seeing things, and then it goes away. There were eighty-five people killed in there, and some of them are still hanging around the casino, at least that's what he told me. He has other friends who've seen it, but they see it kind of out of the corner of their eyes when they're dealing or something. They just kind of see people floating through the casino, not like in the air, but just sort of instead of walking, they're doing this, but they're see-through and it's just for a split second or two, and then they're gone. Whenever you have a catastrophe like that, you're gonna have some ghost activity cause not everybody's gonna want to move on peacefully."

Some insiders even claim that some of those killed by the fire were so angry that they began haunting Kerkorian's new MGM Grand, in a different location. When you consider the circumstances of the tragedy, that really isn't so difficult to believe. Whether they were employees who trusted that their employer would provide a safe workplace or tourists who were in Vegas for the time of their lives, those lives were cut short in a horrifying scene worse than any disaster film dreamed up by Hollywood—all caused, most believe, solely by the extreme greed, impatience, and short-sightedness of the owners of the MGM Grand.

The famed lion statue at the entrance to the MGM Grand. *Photo by Liz Cavanaugh.*

21

THE ALADDIN HOTEL

The Aladdin Hotel has had a complicated and confusing past. Las Vegas folklore says that the property the hotel was built on was jinxed and that anything built on the land was basically doomed from the start. Located between the Flamingo and Tropicana hotels on the Strip's eastern side, the site had been undeveloped desert land until 1963.

The Aladdin Hotel was the first major casino to open on the Las Vegas Strip in the 1960s, eight years after the area's 1950s boom period ended with the opening of the Stardust in 1958. Despite its initial success, the Aladdin would always have a black cloud looming overhead.

Guests at the hotel swear they've heard keys trying to unlock their doors and disembodied voices whispering in the hallways. The key sound is especially interesting since the hotel hasn't used actual keys in several years, just quiet plastic key cards.

Many who have visited have also claimed to "feel" a presence in their rooms and claim that items appeared in their rooms out of nowhere. Even stranger happenings are said to have occurred on the seventh floor in the Panoramic Suite, where the door bell would mysteriously ring and people could be heard talking in the completely empty foyer. Who or what could be causing the chaos? The Aladdin has had many owners and many guests throughout its checkered past, but no one knows for sure.

The Aladdin first opened as the Tally-Ho in 1963. By 1964, the hotel had already undergone its first name change when it became the King's Crown. The new and improved hotel failed within six months of its opening when it was denied a gaming license.

The King's Crown was purchased by Milton Prell in 1966. Renovations and a new five-hundred-seat showroom, called the Bagdad Theater, were added. Some of the original buildings were

The Aladdin Hotel in her hey-day.
Public Domain—courtesy PDPhoto.org.

demolished, and a new section was built. With a new look and new owner, the property was temporarily back on track. The once English-themed hotel quickly evolved into a full-fledged Arabian Nights theme, complete with a fifteen-story "Aladdin's Lamp" neon sign.

The new Aladdin Hotel and Casino opened on April 1, 1966. Guests were greeted with flower petals pouring from the ceiling. The hotel was an instant hit. Prell tried to think of new and innovative ways to entice new gamblers. One notably successful idea was to revamp the typical hotel showroom schedule by featuring three completely different shows twice each night. Within a year, the Aladdin was the toast of the Strip and even played host to the biggest secret wedding event of that era when Elvis wed Priscilla. Coincidently, Prell was close friends with Elvis's longtime manager, Colonel Tom Parker.

By 1969, the hotel had added the famous Sinbad Lounge; it also changed owners again with the Parvin Dohrmann Corporation taking over the reins. In 1972, Sam Diamond purchased the property and the Aladdin underwent a $60 million dollar renovation that added a nineteen-story tower and 7500-seat performing arts center. The hotel also received a new state of the art sign towering 140 feet high and costing over $300 thousand dollars. The hotel reopened again in 1976 with Neil Diamond on hand to perform.

By 1980, part of the hotel was again up for grabs. This time, Mr. Las Vegas, Wayne Newton, bought into the property and remained a part owner from 1980 to 1982. In a telling interview with Newton written by Ed Koch for the *Las Vegas Sun,* Newton tells the story of his involvement with the Aladdin and how it almost ruined his life.

"Newton, one of the top-drawing stars in Las Vegas Strip history, recalled that the Aladdin had become an embarrassment to gaming officials who had to act fast to preserve the integrity of gaming laws in Nevada. That integrity was called into question during the March 1979 sentencing of four Aladdin officials convicted in Detroit of allowing Detroit mobsters to run the resort. While doling out prison terms, U.S. District Judge John Feikens said, "The state of Nevada seems to be reluctant to prosecute offenses committed under its own laws." Feikens noted there was a lack of case references on any similar offenses. In effect, he was saying Nevada was not doing its job to keep the mob out of the gaming industry. "I was working hard to close the deal to buy the Aladdin because I didn't want to see the employees out on the street," Newton said. "It was so irritating. They (the Gaming Commission) gave us thirty days to meet their requirements. When we did, they put in new ones. They wanted the Aladdin closed."

Senator Harry Reid, D-Nev., then-chairman of the Nevada Gaming Commission, said Newton was correct about the board's overall feelings at the time. "We also wanted the employees to remain working, but there was nothing we could do because the place was being run by a bunch of gangsters and the whole world was watching," Reid said. "We really felt compelled to do something drastic." Reid said that, at one point, the gaming commission created the post of receiver to run the resort and keep the employees working, even though there was nothing in the state law to provide for receivership. In August 1979, the state closed the Aladdin, but federal Judge Harry Claiborne ordered it reopened immediately. Eleven months later, gaming officials again closed it. That September, Newton and Ed Torres, the former chief executive officer of the Riviera, bought the resort for $85 million and reopened it the next month.

But it almost did not happen that way, as another world-famous entertainer had a big jump on gaining ownership of the Aladdin. "Mr. (Johnny) Carson and (gaming veteran) Mr. (Ed) Nigro all but had the Aladdin," Newton said. "The previous stockholders had gotten into trouble and had to sell the place, and they were being squeezed. Every time a deal was made, they (the buyers) would change the terms. I was coming off stage at the Sands at two o'clock one morning and a friend called and said, 'Is your ($105 million) offer still on the table?' I said it is, and he said to meet him and the Aladdin stockholders at 8am at the Aladdin. I met (then-Aladdin legal counsel) Sorkis Webbe that morning, and he said, 'Kid, we want you to have the Aladdin.' But it was not so much that they wanted me to own the Aladdin. It was that they were frustrated and wanted anyone but them (Carson and Nigro) to own it. I wanted the Aladdin because I thought I could put a face on it."

Newton said he was at a time in his life when he needed a change. He had worked for the Summa Corp.—the gaming arm of the Howard Hughes Empire—for fourteen years. Also at that time, famed theatrical booking agent Walter Kane, "who was like a father to me, passed away. There was a void in my life," Newton said. "And I opened my big mouth and said I wanted to own a casino, not operate one. I didn't want people coming to me because the toilets are backed up. I wanted owner status. I saw the changes going on in this town with many places doing away with dinner shows. It was different from when I first performed here when I was fifteen."

Newton had looked around. He provided seed money for the Shenandoah Casino that never got off the ground, toured the Edgewater in Laughlin, discussed building a casino in Carson City, and considered the Riviera before targeting the Aladdin. To come up with the purchase price, Newton needed a partner. Torres, who at the time had just sold his interest in the Riviera, fit the bill.

"I was in New York working on getting financing when I got a call informing me that Ed wanted to be my partner," Newton said. "He was my first boss when I came to town and worked at the Fremont. Boy, had I come full circle."

In December, 1979, the Nevada Gaming Commission had voted unanimously to deny a gaming license for Torres and veteran gaming executive Delbert Coleman to purchase the Aladdin. Torres found in Newton a popular individual who had prestige and political clout to make acquisition of the Aladdin possible. But after twenty-one months together, Torres and Newton split. "All of those reports that we were fighting were not true," Newton said. "We never had fights—we had philosophical differences."

The disagreements, Newton said, ranged from reducing the size of shot glasses in the showroom to firing longtime employees—things Newton opposed. But what turned out to be a real big problem, he said, was a disagreement over buying a service station on Las Vegas Boulevard that they would have leveled to give the Aladdin better access to and from the Strip. "The service station owner wanted $6 million," Newton said, noting that he thought the price was okay. "But Ed wouldn't go over $4 million. As a result, it was never bought. It was a mistake. Another problem was that people would call the Aladdin 'Wayne's place,' and I know that bothered Ed. But, like I said, I wanted the Aladdin to have a face."

During ownership of the Aladdin, the pair also had other interests. Torres, who served as the Aladdin's general manager, bought the old Silverbird, now the defunct El Rancho, while Newton was licensed in May 1982 as partner in the Tropicana TraveLodge. In July 1982, Torres bought out Newton for $8.5 million.

Newton said he loved owning the Aladdin. "It was one of the great learning experiences of my life. And I'm one of the few people who owned the Aladdin who can say we made money those years."

The darkest part of his casino ownership days came when reports surfaced that Newton allegedly had ties to the mob. Years earlier, Newton had known Guido Penosi, a reputed member of the Carlo Gambino Mafia crime family of New York. Newton testified several times that he did not know about Penosi's alleged mob ties. "I was most upset with the allegations because my parents were alive, and when my mother saw the report on NBC (in October 1980, linking Newton to organized crime figures), she started crying," Newton said. "I was angry. After that, the stories started coming out that I was a front for the mob at the Aladdin. Later the reports said I was providing the authorities information about the Mafia. It was ridiculous. I'm an Indian boy from Virginia, What do I know about the Mafia?"

It got so bad that Newton's life was threatened because, he said, "The mobsters didn't know that I didn't know anything about them. I was in Los Angeles and got a call from the FBI telling me they would meet me at the (McCarran International) airport to tell me something they couldn't discuss over the phone. They showed me a hit list they had received from an informant. It had five names on it—mine and the names of four guys who already had been killed."

Newton sued NBC and won a $19 million defamation judgment. Later the appeals court ruled that, while the NBC report about Newton was inaccurate, there was no malice. Newton, a public figure, had to prove malice to get damages. He got none. "It was not about money, it was about clearing my name," Newton said. "And I did."

Newton said, at the time that he believed the new Aladdin would succeed where the old Aladdin did not. "I see a tremendous future," he said. "It has a great mystique. It is a great property. A funny thing is that when I was trying to buy back the Aladdin (in 1984-85), I had picked Richard Goeglein (the current Aladdin Gaming chief executive officer) to run it. But then Ginji Yasuda bought the Aladdin and that ended it (Newton's attempted return)."

Fred Lewis, then spokesman for the Aladdin, acknowledges that the current operators have a lot more going for them than Newton and the late Yasuda had. "This is not the same hotel and it is not the same location, even though it is the Aladdin and it is in the same place," he said, "Ginji and Wayne didn't have the Bellagio across the street and the Paris next door. By virtue of not moving, our location has improved."

Newton said he would someday like to own another casino: "Sure, I would love to do it again, but in this day of publicly held companies and mega-resorts, it is very unlikely that I will."

Lynn Holt, another former Aladdin spokesman, said the Aladdin is not ashamed of its colorful past. "It's a fabled history, with Elvis getting married here," Holt said. It is the only Las Vegas hotel-casino ever to be imploded and keep its old name. The Dunes went down in October 1993, and today is the Bellagio. The Landmark came down in November 1995, and today is a parking lot. The Sands was blasted in 1996 and today is the Venetian.

Since Koch's article first appeared, the Aladdin continued until it closed on November 25, 1997. The following year, on April 27, the Aladdin Hotel and Casino was imploded. Only the Aladdin Theater remained.

Three years later, on August 17, 2000, the Aladdin was scheduled to reopen; however, the debut was, as usual, complicated. Public festivities, which included musical acts and fireworks, were scheduled to get underway when the Clark County building inspector delayed the celebration to complete last minute fire safety tests. Shortly thereafter, another delay was caused by a problem with the casino's surveillance system. These complications left spectators disappointed, gamblers frustrated, and hotel guests angry as they wondered where they'd sleep.

The Desert Passage Mall, whose debut was part of the grand reopening, did open on schedule with Barbara Eden (*I Dream of Jeannie*) in her famous pink harem outfit on hand to open the doors. The rest of the Aladdin opened the next morning with around 2,000 Culinary Workers Union Local 225 members and other workers protesting the hotel's opening without a union contract. The casino was never successful and remained in constant financial trouble.

In 2003, new owners again came on the scene when Planet Hollywood and Starwood Hotels & Resorts Worldwide bought the Aladdin. So far, the Planet Hollywood Hotel and Casino is doing well, with expansion underway. The Arabian Nights theme and magic carpets have been replaced with a sleek décor, movie stars, hip bars, and the support of a worldwide franchise.

Some people say that years of organized crime involvement lead to the ultimate demise of the Aladdin; still others blame the land it was built on.

Milton Prell's vision for his hotel was a theme based on the Middle-Eastern folk tale of a boy named Aladdin whose oil lamp contained a genie granting wishes. Perhaps that mystical boy still haunts the property in search of a genie that can save it.

You can see the restored "Aladdin's Lamp" that was part of the original sign at the "Boneyard" on Fremont Street.

22

THE MIRAGE, THE CASTAWAYS, AND THE BATHROOM

Where else but Las Vegas can you find an exact replica of a live volcano that spews fake molten lava and fire every night on the hour? Built by uber entrepreneur Steve Wynn, in 1989, the Mirage hotel was the first hotel on the strip funded by Wall Street. When it was finished, it was the most expensive hotel casino ever built. The hotel had a seven-year construction loan to pay off. In order to do that, the property would have to bring in a million dollars every day, which it did. In fact, revenue from the hotel was so good, they paid off the loan in just eighteen months.

The heart of the Mirage beats in the volcano show. Crowds gather every night at the top of the house to watch the earth rumble and roar until flames and fire erupt and shoot a hundred feet in the air. The sight is spectacular and draws the same oohs and ahhs from the crowds that you hear at a fourth of July fireworks show. Now, almost twenty years after the volcano had its virgin eruption, the MGM Mirage (as it's now called), has poured $25 million into a facelift of the famed attraction. It's hoped that the renovation, which will feature a state of the art sound and water show (designed to rival the dancing fountains of the Bellagio) along with the erupting

The famous erupting volcano at the Mirage. *Public Domain—courtesy PDPhoto.org.*

volcano, will attract a new and younger crowd back to the hotel, which has seen a decrease in popularity in the past few years and is undergoing an internal renovation as well.

The MGM Mirage is still a fine hotel by anyone's standards. From 1990 through 2003, it was the home of Siegfield and Roy and their famed white tigers. When Roy Horn was attacked by one of his tigers during a show in 2003, it resulted in massive injuries for the star, and it was not only the loss of a major attraction but a loss of a huge revenue generator for the hotel. Other current shows on site include Cirque du Soleil's famed Beatle's tribute, *Love*, and headliner Danny Gans. Gans is a former professional baseball player turned musical mega impressionist and a Las Vegas favorite.

So, where do the ghosts hang out in the MGM Mirage? In the bathroom. The bathroom of the Danny Gans Theater, to be exact. Apparently, many of the theater's bathroom visitors have been startled by the sink faucets that somehow turn themselves on and off for no particular reason. Rumor has it that there is even one hotel staffer who refuses to clean the bathroom and carries her rosary each times she passes the scary restroom area.

The site where the MGM Mirage was built was originally the home of the original Castaways Hotel & Casino. Before the Castaway was built, the Red Rooster Nite Club sat on the property. The original club burned down in 1931. The Red Rooster Nite Club was rebuilt, and the San Souci Auto Court was constructed next door. By 1957, the San Souci Auto Court owners added a hotel to the property. Finally, in 1963, the property became the Castaways Hotel & Casino. In 1970, the Castaways was sold to billionaire Howard Hughes for $3 million. It was one of the many properties bought up by the illusive Hughes from 1966 to the mid seventies. The Castaways Hotel & Casino remained open for business until 1987 when Steve Wynn bought the property and tore it down.

There doesn't seem to be a reported history of ghosts haunting any of the previous businesses that operated on the property, which is located at 3400 South Las Vegas Boulevard. So, here's some food for thought. Could a well meaning former patron of the Red Rooster Nite Club be turning on the faucets to help put out the fire?

It is well documented that Howard Hughes was obsessed with germs and suffered from OCD (obsessive compulsive disorder). One of the common symptoms of the disorder is a compulsion to wash your hands, which Hughes did, sometimes up to 100 times per day. Could the ghost of Howard Hughes be lurking around a bathroom in the theater that sits on property he once owned? Could he be turning on the faucets to promote good hygiene with Danny Gan's fans? We'll never know for sure.

Danny Gans puts on a wonderful show, but you may want to avoid the bathroom area of the theater if unpredictable faucets concern you. Regardless, the volcano show out front should be on your "must see" list.

23

THE CURSE
OF THE LUXOR

Ancient Egyptian pyramids were built over 3,000 years ago as tombs for the Pharaohs and their families. When a pharaoh died, he became Osiris or a king of the dead. Ancient Egyptians believed that part of a dead pharaoh's spirit remained with his body. This was known as his *ka*. To prevent a catastrophe, each dead pharaoh's body was mummified for preservation. In an effort to send them off in style, everything a king or pharaoh, or anyone else for that matter, could possibly need was buried in the tomb with them: food and vessels of the finest wines, utensils to prepare meals, furniture, clothing, gold, and jewels, as well as many of their most cherished possessions. Sometimes even an unsuspecting servant was included to make the afterlife as comfortable as possible for their former employer. It was believed that if a corpse did not receive the finest of care, the pharaoh would not be able to carry out his new responsibilities on the other side, possibly bringing great sadness and doom to Egypt.

Today somewhere between 80 and 100 of the Great Pyramids remain. Most are located near Cairo just south of the Nile Delta. Ancient folklore suggests that the pyramids hold great secrets. Over 7,000 miles away, in Las Vegas, Nevada, only one pyramid exists, the Luxor Hotel, and it seems to hold a few secrets of its own. Built in 1993, the Luxor sits at the southern end of the strip at East Reno Ave and Las Vegas Boulevard

South. A giant replica of the Sphinx invites you to enter, or at least stop, and take a photo or two.

Here are some specifics on the property. The hotel is a 350-foot-high, 30-story pyramid. The tip of the pyramid has a fixed position spotlight that shoots straight up to the stars. It is the brightest beam in the world. While this is unique and certainly interesting to look at, rumors of it interfering with aircraft have no factual basis: It isn't located beneath a flight path. It is also said that astronauts can see it from space; this is true, but they can't read a newspaper by its light as many reports have said. The beam's output is rated at 41.5 giga candela. Each spring, moths are attracted to the great beam in masses, making it look like it's snowing over this select spot on the strip.

You don't find elevators in the Luxor. Instead you have inclinators which move you along the inside walls of the pyramid at roughly a thirty-nine degree angle. The hotel atrium is one of the largest in the world and is surrounded at every level by guest rooms. Only short safety walls separate the guests from the lobby.

Once known for its Egyptian-themed décor and museum quality exhibits, the hotel has undergone some serious renovations in the past few years. While the lobby is still filled with beautiful stone and marble sculptures that are situated among massive palm trees, some felt the original Egyptian theme had worn out its welcome and the rooms and casino felt dated. In 2007, the hotel's owners (the MGM Grand/Mirage Group) renovated about eighty percent of the hotel at a cost of a whopping $3 hundred million dollars.

Regular guests were outraged by the changes, most specifically the removal of "the River Nile." The "Nile River Tour" was one of the first mega attractions on the strip. Barge-like ferries carried guests down a river running through the casino level of the hotel, passing the temple of Tamesses II, the Temple of Amun, a variety of artwork and hieroglyphics, and ending at the base of a waterfall that made you wish you had brought along your camera. The ride, while not terribly exciting, was not something you often found inside your average hotel and tourists loved it.

As other new and more exciting options cropped up at nearby hotel properties, management felt it was best to let the river run dry and tailor the hotel to attract more upscale tastes and lure bigger spenders into the casino. At least that's what they said. An unofficial, but far more popular story claims they said they removed the ride because passengers often frightfully reported seeing three ghost-like figures when they entered the river's tunnel. Why would ghosts be hanging around the Luxor?

Maybe because they felt they still had work to do. At least one worker died during the construction of the Luxor, while several other workers were seriously injured while working on the site. Other workers who spent time at the location simply wouldn't go back. It is often said that the Luxor is jinxed.

The unique interior of the hotel has not helped the situation. In the past few years, several people have jumped or fallen to their deaths from the hallways, which resemble long balconies, in front of the doors to the rooms. Police reports confirm two deaths; hotel staffers say there have been more. The most notorious story involves a local "lady of the evening" who jumped to her death from the 24th floor, landing directly in front of the buffet restaurant. To make matter worse, and the story more chilling, she was supposedly HIV positive. As a result, it's said, the Luxor was forced to close down the buffet and move it to another location in the hotel.

While the thought of this woman's suicide and blood spatter is bad enough; the addition of the HIV sidebar is sketchy, although stories have a unique way of changing and becoming more detailed with each telling. The second jumper story involves a young man said to be playing chicken on top of a balcony railing, threatening to jump if his girlfriend wouldn't agree to marry him. The man lost the girl and his life when he lost his grip, falling directly on the front desk as they were checking people in. Luckily, no one else was injured, but one wonders if the guests still checked in?

Besides the construction worker's death and the suicides, the curse of the Luxor has been said to be the reason for a fire that caused serious

The Luxor Pyramid. *Photo by Liz Cavanaugh.*

damage at the Stratosphere. The Luxor was nearing completion when the mysterious fire broke out, although there doesn't really seem to be a logical connection.

Construction of the Luxor began in 1991, and when it opened in 1993, it was the tallest hotel in Vegas. The hotel initially had 2,007 rooms; in 1998 another 2,000 rooms (in two towers) were added along with a theater. Still, despite its splendor, the Luxor has a dark side, a strange feeling that some guests can't explain, that lifts as you pass through the lobby doors into the sunshine.

The hotel is built to approximately three-quarter scale to the Great Pyramid and the lobby is a stunning replica of the temple at Abu Simbel with four colossal statues of Ramses. People love the hotel's large bathrooms, the fabulous spa, the three swimming pools, and easy access to the Excalibur and Mandalay Bay by the tram connecting the three properties. They also love taking pictures in the lobby area.

While most of the photographers are just tourists snapping vacation shots to show their friends and family, many others are there for a different reason. Photos taken in the grand lobby are often filled with spirit orbs and ectoplasm, possibly belonging to the lost souls of the people who died there. Ghost hunters consider the Luxor a Mecca for orb enthusiasts and spirit seekers.

Some believe that the Luxor will continue to be cursed until an artificial eye is placed on the capstone of the pyramid, thus changing the mysterious properties of the pyramid. The Eye of Providence or the all-seeing eye is thought to represent the eye of God keeping watch on humankind. Ironically, the ancient Egyptian city of Luxor, or Thebes, had no pyramids.

Another view with lots of orbs.
Photo by Liz Cavanaugh.

Ramses on his throne. Note orbs in photo. *Photo by Liz Cavanaugh.*

More lobby orbs. *Photo by Liz Cavanaugh.*

Note the giant orb to the right on this lobby view of the Luxor.
Photo Liz Cavanaugh.

The mother of all orbs. *Photo by Liz Cavanaugh.*

Dueling orbs. *Photo by Liz Cavanaugh.*

Orbs, orbs, everywhere! *Photo by Liz Cavanaugh.*

Looking down upon the orb-filled lobby. *Photo by Liz Cavanaugh.*

24

THE EXCALIBUR AND THE DUNES

Not every hotel on the Vegas Strip is haunted or has bragging rights based on ghostly inhabitants. Most hotels do, however, have their share of skeletons in the closets and it isn't uncommon for visitors to go home, have their vacation photos developed and notice a few orbs scattered throughout their prints. Sometimes guests just check out with an uneasy feeling that someone was watching them or was constantly looking over their shoulder.

Located about a mile and a half apart are the Bellagio and the Excalibur Hotels. Before the Bellagio was even a glint in Steve Wynn's eye, the Dunes had its moment in the sun. Sadly, The Bellagio already seems to have a ghost. In July of 2004, actor Justin Pierce was found hanging in his room at the hotel. He was recently married and a new father. He had been in Las Vegas to do a fashion photo shoot, and by all accounts seemed fine. The suicide was a shock to his family, although he left two notes of explanation.

The Dunes Hotel was the tenth resort to open on the Las Vegas Strip. Sadly, a black cloud hung over the property from the start. Once based in Paradise, Nevada, the hotel and casino moved to the strip in 1955, and remained open until January 26, 1993. The Hotel's slogan was "The Miracle in the Desert." Yet no miracle showed up in time to save the Dunes.

The Las Vegas Strip. Note the colorful castle turrets of the Excalibur.
Photo by Liz Cavanaugh.

The Dunes had problems from the start, most of them financial. Its location at the southern end of the Strip isolated it from the main crowds. It made headlines and caused a stir with the State's Legislature when it became the first casino to offer a topless review called Minsky's Follies. The Legislature was none too happy about it, but the show set a record attendance bringing in 16,000 guests the first week. The Legislature rethought its position on such shows when they determined their potential cut of the revenues. The monetary success of the Follies helped keep the ship afloat for many years, but again, the bills began stacking up. The hotel did all it could to become financially stable, including booking the highest paid performers of the day into its showroom, including Frank Sinatra. Multiple expansions provided more rooms to fill with high rollers, but nothing did the trick and the hotel's financial situation went from bad to worse.

At one time it was rumored that Howard Hughes would add the property to his vast Vegas holdings. Hughes already owned the Sands Hotel and the Desert Inn. The Dunes completed what was known as the "Three Kings of Las Vegas" so it made perfect since that Hughes would want the property, but the sale never transpired.

A Japanese investor paid $155 million for the hotel in 1987, but was unable to get it in the black. Finally, in 1992, Steve Wynn purchased the doomed property for just $75 million. It was Wynn that started the popular trend of imploding hotels when he literally brought down the North Tower of the hotel in true Vegas fashion—complete with cannon blasts, fireworks, and media from around the world. Over 200,000 spectators lined the Strip to watch the Dunes take her last bow. For some residents of Vegas, the end of the hotel represented the end of another era, an era when the mob controlled the hotels. That's another chapter.

The enormous Dunes sign, often described as resembling a giant onion, was not removed and was destroyed during the implosion along with the giant palm trees that flanked the casino entrance. At one point, it was said to cost nearly $50 thousand dollars a year to keep the 180-foot symbol lit. The sign was reported to have over 10,000 lights and electric "lava" that erupted through it every minute. Ironically, the statuesque sultan statue had been relegated (by 1985) to a lonely spot on the property's golf course. That same year, the lofty symbol suffered a fatal blow when old wiring in its stomach caught fire. Both would have been wonderful additions to the Boneyard.

The Dunes was once one of the finest and most grand hotels on the Strip. By the time it closed, patrons often complained about feeling cold spots throughout the main hotel tower and in the casino. In the lounge, after hours, guests reported seeing a blue glow and heard voices when no one was there.

The elegant and beautiful Bellagio now stands where the "Miracle in the Desert" once stood. During the construction of the Bellagio, workers found four bags of Dunes casino chips that were apparently buried at the site, someone's way of holding on to a glorious but plagued past.

The Excalibur Hotel is currently owned by the MGM Mirage Group. Named for the mythical sword of King Arthur, the property resembles a castle, complete with dark, dungeon-like hallways, Medieval-themed restaurants and jovial staffers decked out in Renaissance period clothing. Although removed in 2007, it once had an enormous Merlin the Magician peering out on the Strip from a turret window.

The Excalibur was built by the folks that gave Las Vegas Circus Circus, and it was opened in 1990. When it debuted, it was the largest hotel in the world, but the property, like most others in Vegas, soon became dated and the crowds headed to newer properties with hipper rooms and newer attractions. The hotel is still geared toward kids and works hard to lure in a family-friendly clientele; a massive renovation has made the property much more appealing to young and old guest alike with the introduction of what they call "Widescreen Rooms" which feature forty-two inch plasma televisions and high-end amenities including alarm clocks with iPod inputs.

A midway called Fantasy Faire is full of the latest high tech arcade games. If that isn't enough, the whole family can climb aboard the new SpongeBob 4D Special FX Ride, where you can watch SpongeBob Square Pants pursue a runaway pickle in his heartfelt desire to serve up the perfect Krabby Patty. Brave riders are transported to Bikini Bottom for what is trumpeted as the adventure of their lives, complete with wind, bubbles, and scent.

What ghost wouldn't want to hang out there?

Although no one has reported actually seeing the ghost, visitors on the tenth floor of the hotel have reported an eerie feeling of being followed, but when they turn around, no one is there. Others say you hear someone whispering in your ear; you can't make out what they're saying, but it gives you goose bumps.

Although it no longer holds the title of the largest hotel in the world, or even on the Las Vegas Strip, The Excalibur continues to reinvent itself and adapt to changing times and the more sophisticated tastes of today's tourist. Case in point, in June 2007, the hotel contracted with Dick's Last Resort restaurant chain. The iconic figure of Merlin that mysteriously went away in 2007 has been replaced by the restaurant's mascot, "Slick Dick."

So, after a ride with SpongeBob and dinner with Slick Dick, you might head up to the tenth floor of the hotel and snoop around, to see if maybe a friendly ghost will tell you where they stashed Merlin.

25

THE SCARIEST SHOW ON EARTH

ircus Circus opened its doors in October of 1968. You'd be hard pressed to find a similar hotel anywhere, except maybe the one in Reno, which is owned by the same group. If being surrounded by throngs of overly-excited children doesn't scare you to death, the giant clown marquee located at the entrance might. "Lucky," who wields a giant lollipop and curly orange Carrot Top hair, beckons you to enter the chaos. The giant neon sign, weighing in at nearly 120 tons, is about as creepy as anything you'd find in a country cemetery at 3am.

Circus Circus is a themed hotel and casino located at the northern end of the Las Vegas Strip. It was originally owned by Jay Sarno, but today the property (along with its sister property in Reno) is just another acquisition among the vast holdings of the MGM Mirage Group.

For more than twenty years, Circus Circus was the only game in town for parents that wanted to drag their kids along to Sin City. Hidden away under a giant red and white striped tent-like building was a whimsical city. Complete with exciting carnival rides, a midway where you could try your luck at games and win a prize, trapeze artists, and clowns that performed several shows each day, it was a kid's paradise. It still is.

Today, the property continues to please with pizza stands, a cantina, fast-food chain restaurants, and a seemingly endless buffet. Parents can play along with their kids on the midway or they can hit the casino, browse the shops, dine at a four-star steakhouse, or sip a cool drink in one of the lounges. Quite literally, Circus Circus does its best to please every kid of every age.

Rounding out this fantasy destination is an indoor theme park. The Adventuredome features the Canyon Blaster, a double-loop, double-corkscrew roller coaster not designed for the faint of heart. The Midway is also where you'll find the famous Horse-Around Bar, the revolving carousel immortalized by Hunter S. Thompson in *Fear and Loathing in Las Vegas*.

While the property seems like a happy vacation spot, alive with the shrieks of happy children, it has its darker side, too. Reports of cries, frightening screams, and other strange noises have surfaced over the years. Hotel guests in several different rooms claim to have heard terrifying screams for help coming from their bathrooms at night. Others have reported hearing faint cries for help coming from the poker room, although a player that just lost his shirt might be a more plausible explanation.

Another well known rumor, based on the accounts of a former employee from one of the hotel's restaurants, claims that three people were murdered one night in one of the kitchens and their ghosts still roam the buildings. Police logs show no record of these murders. Still another story claims a young mother shot her son while staying at the hotel in room 123. She then turned the gun on herself and committed suicide. Supposedly, the mother and child still roam the hotel looking for the child's father and asking for help. Again, no police reports seem to be available to substantiate this claim. Reports of this nature sometimes have an interesting habit of disappearing from public records. Still, the story is sad and chilling.

Circus Circus has the only KOA (Kampgrounds of America) RV park on the Strip providing additional accommodations for nearly 400 campers. Many of them have reported hearing strange sounds and feeling their motor homes shake during the night. Thinking there might have been a slight earthquake nearby, campers awake only to discover there wasn't any report of quake activity during the night.

In 1997, renovations and overall property improvement upgraded the hotel's theme from the standard American circus to a Québec's Cirque du Soleil-type circus. They also added a new thirty-five-story tower. The colorful complex has been the backdrop for several Hollywood films including, James Bond's *Diamonds Are Forever* and *Austin Powers: International Man of Mystery*.

Each October, Circus Circus dresses up in its ghoulish best for Halloween. Ranked as one of the top five scariest haunts in the nation and the only one on the Las Vegas Strip, The Circus Circus Fright Dome is a sight to both beware of and behold. Comprised of five different haunted houses under the big top, the production is pure Vegas and not necessarily suited to young children. Thrill seekers from all over the world flock to the Fright Dome each year for one week only (preceding Halloween) to be scared out of their wits!

These days, the Las Vegas rumor mill is in full swing, hinting that the new owner of the property, the MGM Mirage Group, may demolish the current hotel complex and rebuild. The reasoning is that the Circus Circus site "does not make economic use of the forty-four acres that it sits on." The statement went on to say they would consider keeping the name and theme intact and rebuilding at a new location. One wonders if the ghostly presences would move to a new location or stay where they are and haunt any new buildings on the same site?

Most hotel properties, at one time or another, have guests who report seeing or hearing something that made them uncomfortable or spooked. The reported cries for help coming from different locations around the resort might merit further investigation if there are any ghost hunters ready to pack up and join the circus.

26

SUICIDES IN SIN CITY

Among Vegas' more notorious titles is a very sad one: Suicide Capital of the World. A recent study published in the *Social Science and Medicine* journal by sociology professor Matt Wray of Temple University claimed that Vegas has a higher suicide rate than any other city in the world. It also said that Vegas' tourists commit suicide at an even higher rate than its residents, and that resident suicide lessens when Vegas' inhabitants travel out of town. As expected, gambling losses top the reasons for the deaths. Another cause seems to be the feelings of isolation created in this fastest-rising city in America by those moving away from their support systems of family and friends.

Many of the hotels in town, with varying degrees of success, have covered up the fact that some of their guests have purposefully ended their lives there. Sometimes it can't be hidden, though. Although the hotels and casinos aren't anxious to publicize the suicides they've unwittingly hosted, it's an inescapable fact that those suicides have occurred with an alarming frequency in the city.

There are several "suicide destinations" around the world. Another city with a high suicide reputation is San Francisco, home to the Golden Gate Bridge, where more than 1,000 people have jumped to their deaths since the bridge was constructed in 1937. It averages about twenty suicides a year.

The Stratosphere looms tall above the city.
Photo by Liz Cavanaugh.Cav

The Stratosphere Hotel and Casino is a unique hotel and casino owned by American Casino & Entertainment Properties which is a wholly owned subsidiary of American Real Estate Partners. The property's signature attraction is the 1,149-foot Stratosphere Tower, the tallest free-standing observation tower in the United States and the second tallest in the Western Hemisphere. It is the tallest structure of any kind in Nevada. The hotel and casino complex is in a separate building with approximately 20 stories, 2,444 rooms and an 80,000-square-foot gambling area.

The Stratosphere reigns at the northern most end of the Strip, but is visible from almost anywhere in the city. Following its completion in 1996, it was initially less popular than first envisioned due to its location on the extreme north end of the strip, far away from the most popular hotel casinos. However, its low room prices and unique offerings eventually ensured its success. While many tourists consider its location to be inconvenient, others feel the location is an advantage since it is conveniently located between the Strip and Fremont Street.

In the early 1990s, The Stratosphere was conceived by Bob Stupak to replace his Vegas World casino. In the 1980s, Stupak's Vegas World was highly profitable due to its extensive out-of-state marketing and unique promotions and giveaways. Vegas World easily grossed over one hundred million per year.

At the conception of the Stratosphere, one of the planned rides was to be a giant ape that would carry riders up and down one of the tower's columns. Thankfully, the ape idea tanked. Original plans also called for the Stratosphere to tower over 1,800 feet tall, which would make it, at that time, the world's tallest building. However, due to possible interference with flights landing at nearby McCarran International Airport, the tower's height never reached Stupak's dream.

On August 29, 1993, the tower caught fire while still under construction, causing a gigantic setback for Stupak and the construction of the tower. It was severe enough to close Vegas World, the adjacent resort next to the tower, and caused a crane to list to the side, almost collapsing to the street below. Nobody was injured, but the fire forced repairs and rebuilding that led to numerous delays in the construction of the tower.

The Stratosphere opened on April 30, 1996. Shortly after opening, Bob Stupak's Stratosphere Corporation was forced to file for bankruptcy. The story of Bob Stupak is a fascinating one and could easily fill the pages of a book entirely on its own. An innovative entrepreneur, he's also a highly-skilled poker player who has accumulated almost a million dollars in winnings. Though Stupak no longer owns the Stratosphere, he continues to be a maverick within the community and the state and he has several other projects on the drawing board.

The Stratosphere draws thrill seekers from all over the world; the tower features three of the most frightening rides imaginable. Ever played on a giant teeter-totter, 866 feet above the ground? Meet the X-Scream, a space-age design resembling a massive teeter-totter. The X-Scream propels several riders head-first, 27 feet over the edge of the Stratosphere Tower. After being shot over the edge, riders dangle weightlessly above the Las Vegas Strip before being pulled back and propelled over again for more.

The second of the fright trio is named the Big Shot. The ride shoots thrill seekers 160 feet in the air at 45 miles per hour. In a matter of seconds, the Big Shot thrill ride catapults 16 riders from the 921-foot high platform up the Tower's mast to a height of 1,081 feet and down again. Before having a chance to catch your breath, you'll be shot back up again. Riders experience a gut-wrenching four 'G's of force on the way up, and feel negative 'G's on the way down as your legs dangle in the Las Vegas skyline. This ride is not for the faint of heart.

The third ride is ironically called "Insanity the Ride." A massive mechanical arm extending out 64 feet over the edge of the Stratosphere Tower at a height of over 900 feet, Insanity will spin you and several other passengers in the open air at speeds of up to three 'G's. You'll be propelled up to an angle of 70 degrees, which will tilt your body into one position—facing straight down. It's inadvisable to eat within a couple of hours before braving any of the rides.

Another view of the Stratosphere. *Photo by Liz Cavanaugh.*

Unbelievably long lines of people patiently wait to purchase tickets to experience the adrenaline rush of the Tower rides; others buy a ticket with another purpose in mind.

In March of 2005, Melanie Bell, 36, a television producer from Birmingham, Alabama, jumped to her death from the top of the Stratosphere where she was taking part in a reality show called *Vegas Elvis* that featured the film crew as part of the taping. Bell leaped to her death after asking, "Has anyone jumped off that building before?"

The day she died, Bell was to meet executive producer Chris Dryer of Dream Factory, a Los Angeles-based production company. Dryer got a call from Bell saying the car she was using was on the fourth floor parking lot at the Stratosphere and the keys were at the front desk. He knew exactly what that meant and immediately called security, but it was too late. Security cameras have her on video buying a ticket to the observation deck at 9:40.

The night before, Bell had posed with cast and crew at the Welcome to Las Vegas sign on Las Vegas Boulevard.

She said she was a former showgirl and had put on weight; her friends say she was suffering from anorexia at the time of her death. The Stratosphere is well known for its suicides.

In 2006, a British tourist was celebrating an $11 hundred roulette win. The 27-year-old parcel delivery worker had sent his mother a postcard the day before telling her what a great time he was having and that he was having a run of good luck. On the card he noted, "As you know, I am sensible, so I won't blow my savings..." The next day he jumped off the Stratosphere's Tower. Family members felt he had never really dealt with the suicide of his father which occurred when he was six years old. He left no note.

Recently a 19-year-old boy, who seemed to simply be enjoying his ride, calmly unfastened his safety harness and jumped. He was reported riding the "Big Shot." Family and friends were stunned and confused and had no idea as to why he jumped.

A man from Utah borrowed his girlfriend's car and headed to Vegas; he emptied his bank accounts and maxed out three credit cards before purchasing a ticket to the top of the Tower and jumping off.

A 16-year-old boy scaled the double security fences, slipping past the security guards, and dove head first towards the pavement below. He landed on the parking garage. He had an argument with his parents in another part of the hotel prior to buying a ticket and heading to the tower. His autopsy showed drugs in his system.

There are reportedly several ghosts that lurk around the hotel. One particular ghost, that has been seen several times around the parking garage, is thought to be that of the 16-year-old jumper. He is seen briefly darting from place to place, yet not disturbing any cars or drivers. Another ghost, thought to be the man from Utah, is often seen riding the hotel escalators. He begins to appear in the middle of the escalator and seemingly vaporizes before reaching the top.

There have been five reported suicides there in the past few years; hotel insiders say there could be as many as eight, noting that some stories have a way of missing the final edition of the paper. Regardless, it's easy to sense the lost souls surrounding you as you ponder the view below from the top of the Tower.

If someone is determined to take their own life, they'll find a way. Sadly, the Tower at the Stratosphere has, unintentionally, given them some assistance.

Not far from the Stratosphere is the Oasis Motel. It would take you less than a minute to drive between the two properties. In some regards, the hotels are worlds apart; unfortunately, they have a common denominator. In its hey-day the Oasis was considered to be a nice little motor inn where you could get a clean, reasonably priced room, slightly away from the hectic pace of The Strip. Today, very little has changed cosmetically at the Oasis. Long overdue for a renovation, it's now just another old low-budget motel in desperate need of a face lift, offering little more than a cheap night's sleep, color television, and air conditioning.

Situated at 1731 Las Vegas Boulevard South, the Oasis Motel could easily be overlooked due to its location, lack of amenities,

The welcoming front sign of the Oasis Motel. *Photo by Liz Cavanaugh.*

and a hand-painted sign, but for some, mainly ghost hunters, it's high on their Vegas "must see" list.

In fairness, don't be quick to judge this book by her cover. Despite her outdated outer appearance, the Oasis has a loyal

clientele. Management and staff do their best to make sure the property is cared for and the rooms are clean. It's a dinosaur, a no-frills establishment lost in a sea of excess and glitz. The motel still offers adult movie channels and mirrors on the walls, and it's

rumored that you can get a room for a couple of hours as opposed to just a nightly rate, but keep in mind that at one time, every hotel and motel on the Strip tried this ploy to lure in guests. After all, they do call it Sin City.

The Oasis, however, is well known for another reason.

World-renowned poker player Stu "The Kid" Ungar, who won Binion's Horseshoe World Series of Poker three times and earned millions of dollars gambling, was found dead in the Oasis Motel on November 22, 1998.

Ungar was a professional poker and gin rummy player, widely considered to have been the greatest Texas hold 'em and gin rummy player of all time. Besides his three-time run as winner of the Binion's World Series of Poker, he was the only person to win Amarillo Slim's Super Bowl of Poker three times, the world's second most prestigious poker title during its time.

The sign on the side of the Oasis Motel.
Photo by Liz Cavanaugh.

Tragically, Ungar was found in a single room of the Oasis Motel with about $800 in his pocket. Some personal documents were found in the room, but nothing else. He left no note. Ungar and his ex-wife, Madeline, had a daughter, Stefanie. When they married, Ungar legally adopted Madeline's son from her first marriage, Richie, who took Ungar's surname. Richie committed suicide shortly after his high school prom, devastating both Madeline and Stu. They divorced in 1986.

The famed poker master was alone when he checked into a $58 room on a Saturday night. Ungar signed his name in the motel guest log but listed no home address. Instead, he simply wrote down a phone number for The Mirage. He was found by motel employees about 11am, shortly after checkout time.

Friends and colleagues feared Ungar's addiction to illegal drugs finally killed him. An autopsy showed traces of drugs in his system, but not enough to have directly caused his death. The medical examiner concluded that he had died of a heart condition brought on by his years of drug abuse, but others aren't so sure.

Peter Alson, the co-author of Ungar's biography, said Ungar was the Jim Morrison of poker. "With his hollowed cheeks and surly pout, Ungar looked the part of the romantic rebel. And having become a pet of the extended Genovese crime family after honing his skills in the shadowy card parlors of New York of the 1960s, as his biography recounts, he embraced the wise-guy swagger."

Despite winning millions during his poker career, Ungar died with no assets to his name. Friend and fellow poker player Bob Stupak took up a collection at Ungar's funeral to raise funds to pay for the services. Many of Ungar's friends and fellow competitors said that they thought that he would not live to see his 40th birthday. They were close, Ungar died at age 45 when he was found dead in room 20 at the Oasis.

On Sunday March 21, 1999, actor David Strickland was in Las Vegas hanging out and partying with his buddy, comic actor Andy Dick. At around 1am, the two were spotted enjoying themselves at the famed Glitter Gulch Strip Club. After leaving the Club, Strickland checked into room 20 at the Oasis. Why he chose the Oasis is a mystery. Strickland was one of the stars of the hit television series *Suddenly Susan* and had even dated its star, Brooke Shields; he could have afforded a room at any hotel on the Strip. Strickland put the $55 dollar room charge on his American Express card. Several published interviews with motel owner Peter Napoli confirm that Strickland was alone when he checked in between 3:30 and 4am.

Shortly after checking in, Strickland went to a nearby 7-11 and bought a six pack of Coors. Some reports claim that Strickland returned to the hotel and briefly spoke with a "lady" who was hanging around the motel's courtyard. Unsubstantiated reports go on to say he even invited the woman into his room for a brief stay.

The suicide suite, room 20. *Photo by Liz Cavanaugh.*

At some point late that night, Strickland drank his beer and lined the bottles up on his nightstand. He then removed a king-sized

sheet from the bed, tied it into a noose and secured it over a ceiling beam. Climbing on a chair, still dressed in his jeans, khaki shirt and

sneakers, he placed the noose around his neck and kicked away the chair.

When he didn't check out by 10:30 the following morning, the hotel staff phoned his room. After no answer, an employee with the master key went into room 20 and found him hanging there. Paramedics quickly arrived on the scene, cut him down and unsuccessfully tried to revive him. There were no drugs or additional alcohol found in the room; there was also no note.

Strickland reportedly suffered from bipolar disorder and had a history of drug and alcohol abuse. He was arrested in October 1998 for the possession of cocaine, pleaded no contest in December, was sentenced to thirty-six months probation, and was ordered into rehabilitation. He was due in court on the day of his death for a progress report.

The producers of *Suddenly Susan* decided to deal with Strickland's death in a rather

Another view of room 20.
Photo by Liz Cavanaugh.

unique way. Strickland's character, Todd Stites, simply did not show up to work one day. When Susan, played by Brooke Shields, called him regarding tickets to a show, his pager vibrated on his desk. Susan spends the day searching for Todd, finding out about a number of good deeds he did throughout his life that Susan had no idea about. As the episode comes to an end, the police visit Susan and the office staff as she asks hopefully if they know where Todd is. The exact details of Todd's fate are left ambiguous. His death saddened castmates and friends. Strickland was just twenty-nine years old and by all accounts had a promising acting career ahead of him.

Ghost hunters and paranormal experts concur that room 20 at the Oasis is haunted. Spirit orbs and mist have shown up in numerous room photos taken by the brave souls who have booked themselves into the room for the night. Guests frequently complain that someone is pacing back and forth in the rooms above them, which would be the second floor. Problem is, there is no second floor. The Oasis is a one level complex with all rooms on the ground level.

Some guests have checked out after seeing clothes hangers fly out of the closets and zip around the room while the bathroom faucets turn on and off. Other guests have often reported hearing moaning coming from room 20 when staying on either side of it. The moaning sounds painful, not pleasurable.

27

GHOSTS
OF OLD CASINOS

North of "The Strip" is the Las Vegas Motor Speedway, a $200 million dollar complex which sits like a diamond in the desert. It is one of the most complete racing complexes in the world with its 1,600 acres, which includes road courses, a three-eighths mile oval, a dirt track, and a state-of-the-art drag racing facility. Cars whiz by so fast they seem like just a blur. It reminds one a little of the hotels and casinos on the Strip. Las Vegas is continuously reinventing itself and the list of casino sales, implosions, name changes, and closures is a permanent work in progress at an alarming rate.

Sometimes unlucky tourists, using outdated websites and unscrupulous travel agents, find themselves booked at a hotel with no vacancy. Below is a list of hotels you might want to avoid, not necessarily because they're haunted, simply because they no longer exist. The following is the most recent recap of closings, name changes, and implosions at the writing of this book. You might want to refer to this list before you book your next trip.

Big Red's Casino: Closed in 1982, turned into Sports World Casino, closed in 2001; this is now a shopping center.

Boardwalk Casino: Demolished May 9, 2006, will become CityCenter. Expect completion 2010.

Bonanza Casino: Demolished, opened in 1973 at the MGM Grand, in 1985 changed into Bally's.

Boomtown Casino: Changed name to Silverton in 1998.

Bourbon Street Casino: Closed in 2005, now vacant.

Castaways Casino: Closed and imploded in 2005.

Continental Casino: Closed in 1999, remodeled and opened in 2000 as Terrible's Casino.

Debbie Reynolds Casino: Sold in 1998 to the World Wrestling Federation, renamed the Convention Center Drive Hotel, sold in 2000 and renamed Greek Isles Casino in 2001.

Desert Inn Casino: Sold to Howard Hughes in 1967, changed hands a couple more times, and then in 1993, sold to ITT/Sheraton, sold again in 1998 to Starwood Hotels, sold to Steve Wynn in 2000, closed in 2001, partially imploded in October 2001. The balance was demolished in 2004, and is now part of Wynn Las Vegas.

Dunes Casino: Demolished in 1993, now is the Bellagio Casino.

El Rancho Vegas: Burned in 1960, now is the Hilton Grand Vacation Club, with a timeshare on part of the land.

El Rancho Casino: Closed in 1992, demolished in 2000, after being sold to Turnberry Associates.

Fiesta Casino: Sold to Station Casinos in 2001, name changed to Fiesta Rancho.

Frontier Casino: In 1967, sold to Howard Hughes, sold to Margaret Elardi in 1988, sold again to Phil Ruffin in 1998 and renamed the New Frontier. The New Frontier closed its doors at 12am on July 16, 2007, and was demolished on November 13, 2007.

Gold Strike Casino: Sold to Circus Circus in 1995, name change to Mandalay Resort Group in 1999, then in 2004 became part of the Merger with MGM Mirage.

Hacienda: Demolished in 1996, is now the Mandalay Bay Casino.

Holy Cow Casino Cafe and Brewery: Closed in 2002.

Jackpot Casino: Closed in 1977, is now part of the Sahara.

Key Largo Casino: Closed in 2005.

Klondike Casino: Closed in 2006, soon to be demolished.

Landmark Casino: Closed in 1991, demolished in 1995 and is now part of the Las Vegas Convention Center Parking Structure.

Las Frontier Casino: Opened in 1942 and renamed to New Frontier in 1955.

Le Reve Casino: Was the working name for what is now Wynn Las Vegas. It never opened under the working name.

Lotus Inn Casino: Closed in 1978, is now a Rodeway Inn.

Lucky Slots Casino: Closed in 1981, is now a retail shopping center.

Marina Casino: Closed in November 1991, in December 1993 is now part of the MGM Grand.

Maxim Casino: Sold in 1998, sold several more times and in 2002 sold to Columbia Sussex Corp, remodeled and in 2003 opened as Westin Casuarina Hotel.

Mint Casino: Sold in 1989 and become part of Binion's Horseshoe.

Money Tree Casino: Closed in 1979.

Nevada Palace Casino: Opened in July 1979 and changed hands in 1983. It is now part of the parking lot of the Eastside Cannery Casino, which opened in late 2008.

New Frontier Casino: From 1955 to 1967, then changed name to Frontier.

Nob Hill Casino: Closed in 1990, is now Casino Royale.

Paddlewheel Casino: Closed in 1991, opened in 1993 as the Debbie Reynolds which closed in 1996 and is now the Greek Isles Casino.

Reserve Casino: Sold in 2001 to Station Casinos and the name changed to Fiesta Henderson.

Royal Nevada Casino: Opened in 1955, changed name in 1958 to Stardust.

San Souci: Closed in 1962, made into the Castaways, and then demolished in 1987, is now The Mirage.

San Remo Casino: Sold in 2004, changed the name to Hooters.

Sands Casino: Demolished in 1996, is now The Venetian.

Showboat Casino: Sold in 2000, changed name to Castaways, sold several times and in 2005 closed and demolished.

Silver City Casino: Closed in 1999, is now the Silver City Shopping Center.

Silver Nugget Casino: Name change in 1990 to Mahoney's Silver Nugget.

Silver Slipper: Demolished in 1988, made into a parking lot and now the Desert Inn Road Arterial.

Silverbird Casino: Sold in 1981 and renamed El Rancho.

South Coast Casino: Sold and name change in October 2006, new name is South Point.

Stardust Resort & Casino: Closed November 1, 2006, demolished March 13, 2007, will become Echelon Place, expect completion in 2010.

Tally Ho Hotel: (Legal name was King's Crown Tally Ho) Sold in 1966, turned into The Aladdin, which in 2006 became Planet Hollywood.

Thunderbird Casino: Closed in 1976, reopened as Silverbird.

Treasury Casino: Sold and renamed as the San Remo in 1989.

Union Casino: Opened in 1970, renamed in 1971 as Union Plaza Casino.

Vegas World: Sold in 1994, demolished in 1995, is now the Stratosphere.

Westward Ho Casino: Closed in 2005, demolished in 2006.

Vacation Village Resort & Casino: Closed in 2002, sold in 1994 to Turnberry Assoc., demolished.

28

THE BONEYARD

Once upon a time there was a beautiful lady's silver slipper that lived high above Las Vegas in a neon silhouette against the sky. Howard Hughes was convinced that the government was spying on him and doing it by hiding a camera in the toe of that giant lady's shoe. The same shoe that gracefully shimmered in hundreds of brilliant lights, complete with a fashionable bow, was mounted high above the sign at the legendary Silver Slipper Hotel and Casino. The reason Hughes was convinced the shoe was being used to watch him was because the sparkling toe of the shoe pointed directly towards Hughes's suite at the Desert Inn. There was never any proof that the camera existed, but Hughes was paranoid and bought the Silver Slipper to make sure the famed giant shoe was in his court. The Hotel and Casino are long gone, but not the glorious Silver Slipper!

Las Vegas is universally known for its glitz, glitter and extreme excess; it's also known as the neon capital of the world. The signs that light up the hotels and casinos on the strip are as well known as the entertainers that grace the showrooms. Using more than 15,000 miles of neon tubing and millions of individual light bulbs, they say that astronauts can see the lights of Las Vegas from space. Ever wonder about what happens to these gigantic neon cultural icons when a property is sold or renovated? They go to where all good signs go: The Boneyard.

The Neon Museum, which opened in November of 1996, offers up a three-acre lot, known as The Boneyard, which is chock full of old signs

Ready to Write a Book?

Are you fascinated by the paranormal? Do you turn the conversation at every dinner party toward the otherwordly? Are you ready to share all the stories you've heard, and to investigate further?

We're eagerly seeking authors to pen local ghost story books. If this idea appeals to you, we'd love to hear more. Email your book idea to:

info@schifferbooks.com or write to Acquisitions, Schiffer Publishing, Ltd. 4880 Lower Valley Rd., Atglen, PA 19310, or call 610-593-1777 to make an appointment to speak with an editor.

Welcome to fabulous downtown Las Vegas. *Photo by Liz Cavanaugh.*

from hotels, casinos, restaurants, dry cleaners, flower shops, and a fabulous array of old night club signs—the same signs you remembered seeing in magazine and old newsreels enticing you to come to visit Vegas. It's a trip down memory lane dotted with artistically significant souvenirs of a different era and a wonderful place to visit.

According to their website, the mission statement of the Neon Museum is to "collect, preserve, study, and exhibit neon signs and associated artifacts to inspire educational and cultural enrichment for diverse members of our international community." Their motto is simple: Repair, Restore, and Remember.

All of the signs and other notable memorabilia have been given to the museum or loaned by sign companies and individual owners or the businesses that once proudly displayed them. This neon collection has signs dating back to the 1940s. Some pieces have been restored; others are exactly the way they arrived.

Many familiar iconic signs are currently on display including the old 5th Street Liquor sign. Circa 1946, the sign illuminated the downtown establishment until it's closing in 1988. The very first sign the museum showcased was the refurbished "Hacienda Horse and Rider" which is still on display along with the sign from Dot's Flowers, a well-known local floral shop on Las Vegas Boulevard. Aladdin's Lamp which was originally installed at the Aladdin Hotel back in 1966 as well as "Andy Anderson," the famous Anderson Dairy mascot, are also part of the treasure trove.

In 2000, the museum received the original martini glass sign from the famed Red Barn. You can also see several signs from various Binion properties, the skull that used to be a part of the Treasure Island Resort, The Stardust sign and bits and pieces of the wonderful old entrance sign from the Golden Nugget. When Steve Wynn renovated the hotel in 1984, he decided that the sign had to go. Residents complained, but their complaints fell on deaf ears. The sign was once the most recognizable in the city. One of the Neon Museum's current projects involves restoring the La Concha Motel Lobby sign, designed by the internationally known architect Paul Revere Williams.

Fans of the CBS hit series *CSI* may recall an episode where the team investigated a body found on the "W" from the original Showboat Hotel and Casino. There are stray letters from many of hotel signs strewn throughout the Boneyard.

There is a little bit of everything at the museum, and you're welcome to snap as many photos as you'd like for your personal enjoyment. They do allow professional photographers to come in and use the property as a back drop for shoots, but this, of course, needs to be arranged in advance with the fee negotiated ahead of time. Be warned, all visits, tours, and shoots are subject to cancellation due to construction and new sign deliveries.

One famous sign you won't find in the Boneyard is the "Welcome to Fabulous Las Vegas" sign. A world-wide icon and fixture of the Strip since 1959, the sign was commissioned by commercial artists Betty Willis and Ted Rogich for Clark County, Nevada. Willis

A long-gone marquee sign. *Photo by Liz Cavanaugh.*

received $4,000 for her original design. Ironically, the county failed to place a copyright on the sign's design which is why you see it freely reproduced on every souvenir you can think of and then some.

The original sign is located at Las Vegas Boulevard approximately one mile south of Tropicana Avenue just past Mandalay Bay. Taking photos of the sign has always been a dangerous proposition for tourists, but that will soon change. In September of 2008, it was officially announced that Clark County broke ground on a twelve-space parking lot abutting the east side of Las Vegas Boulevard. The lot will have twelve slots (including two handicapped spaces) with an additional area reserved for busses. City fathers hope the new parking area will give tourists a safe zone for taking their photos.

Still, if you can't get a good shot of the sign, you do have other options. A second sign saying "Welcome to Fabulous Downtown Las Vegas" is just within the city limits on Las Vegas Boulevard. And, if you still can't get your shot, try the one installed in 2006 located in the center meridian of Boulder Highway near Harmon Avenue. If you've never seen the signs and are curious, the letter "o" in the word "Welcome" is actually a small silver dollar while the back of each sign says "Drive Carefully, Come Back Soon!" As unimaginable as it sounds, the original sign had its plug pulled for almost a month back in 1999 when the company that had been paying the bill was bought out by another firm. The new owners didn't pay the bill. Eventually, the problem was resolved and the past due bill was paid. The delinquent amount that caused the entire problem was less than $60.

The ghosts of old Las Vegas are everywhere and, if you look real close, you might just see a spirit orb or two peeking out from behind the "Welcome to Fabulous Las Vegas" sign in your photos. If not, you'll probably catch your share in the photos you take back at the Boneyard while you take a walking tour of the Neon Museum. Don't forget that you'll need to make a reservation in advance. Located at 821 Las Vegas Boulevard North, it's just a short distance from where many of their artifacts were proudly displayed in their younger days. Right now you can get up close and personal to the signs; eventually the museum hopes to move them to a permanent indoor display area. The Neon Museum main office is located in the Reed Whipple Cultural Center. Their exhibition is considered to be the display of antique signs scattered around the

Freemont Street area. The Boneyard is located a short walk further north. The Neon Museum exhibits are free while the Boneyard cost around $15 for a two-hour walking tour.

If the signs seemed huge when they were in use back in their heyday, wait until you see how big they are when you stand next to them! The museum is run by terrific people. The tour is entertaining, educational, and worth every penny, and at night the signs are lit up and shine in all their neon light glory. New signs and treasures are constantly being acquired, and the museum will continue to expand as long as Vegas developers keep tearing down old properties and renovating existing ones.

Recently, The Neon Museum formed a new partnership with the Old Las Vegas Mormon Fort State Historic Park (commonly known as the Old Fort.) The Old Fort currently displays signs in its visitor's center. The signs you'll see at the Old Fort include the elegantly restored icon from Society Cleaners with its top hat and cane. The sign was a landmark in the Fremont Street area where it stood for sixty years.

The official website of Las Vegas, Vegas.com, gives a colorful, dead on description of the Boneyard. "The easiest way to describe the feeling you get inside the fences at the Neon Boneyard is to imagine a giant shoe. A shoe that is bigger than your refrigerator, a shoe bigger, or so it seems, than the tiny space of your first apartment. Imagine this shoe covered in light bulbs and peeling metallic-colored paint, sitting in the middle of a dusty lot in downtown Las Vegas. Staring up at it, you realize your own shoe, the one strapped to your foot and tied with sloppy knots, isn't even big enough to be an annoying piece of gum stuck to this giant shoe. Meet the Silver Slipper. Weighing in at two tons and towering fifteen feet high, it's one of the first indications you're among giants."

The slipper, a relic from the casino of the same name, and its more than 150 friends make up the Neon Boneyard, which in turn makes up a large part of the Neon Museum, which in turn makes up a Goliath-size chunk of Las Vegas history. And that's what happened to the wonderful silver slipper.

When you get home, look for the spirit orbs in your photographs that may have attached themselves to the old neon landmarks.

29

GHOSTS OF THE FUTURE

L as Vegas is a city in continuous motion: constantly building, renovating, and making everything in sight bigger, better, and more garish then it was before. While the nonstop demand for qualified construction workers makes Las Vegas a good place to find employment, it can also be a dangerous place to work. The building pace is fast and furious, and missed deadlines are costly and dangerous.

Point in case, since 2006, eleven workers have died working on various construction sites located on the Strip. Workers often complain that speed is emphasized over safety, and many find themselves untrained and unskilled for the tasks at hand. As with any growing city, deaths have occasionally occurred over the years as Las Vegas blossomed and matured. However, as the city fought to remain competitive, the number of construction related deaths has climbed well above the national average.

One major project, the MGM Mirage's CityCenter, has seen six workers die since the project got underway in 2006. The CityCenter, slated to open in late 2009, is not just another splashy hotel set to adorn the Strip. When completed, it will be a city within a city, boasting million dollar condos, hotels, high-end shopping, cinemas, four-star restaurants, and, of course, a state-of-the-art casino to rival all the others in town.

The CityCenter is one of, if not the most, expensive privately funded construction projects ever attempted in U.S. history, with estimates that the final tab will come in at over ten billion dollars. At any given time, there are between 4,000 and 8,000 workers on the property to insure that it becomes the most grand not only in the city, but in the West.

OSHA (Occupational Safety and Health Administration) officials have conducted extensive safety inspections at the site and are looking into the deaths of the workers. Other union-affiliated organizations are doing the same. However, those familiar with the project fear that more workers will be lost if the pace of the giant undertaking isn't slowing down. Whether or not that will happen remains to be seen. Reportedly, the MGM Mirage could lose a bonus fee of $100 million for not completing the project on time. This supposed bonus fee is from their partner, DubaiWorld. DubaiWorld kicked in about five billion to buy half stakes in the project and a small percentage of the MGM Mirage.

The MGM Mirage issued a public statement after one of the latest fatalities claiming, "Workplace safety is the joint responsibility of the contractor's subcontractors and unions; in practice, however, safety can only be assured by individuals."

In fairness, the MGM Mirage organization is vast and reputable. As an employer, it largely provides thousands of people with a place to work, insurance, and a decent income. Its properties are favorites among the throngs of tourists that flock to the city each year.

In the meantime, the city watches and waits in hopes that the recent deaths on the CityCenter site will be the last. Sadly, some residents have begun to refer to the CityCenter as "City Cemetery."

Will any of these workers who were killed haunt the site once it is complete? It has been known to happen before.

30

TOUR OPERATOR ROBERT ALLEN KNOWS HIS VEGAS GHOSTS

Robert Allen is a stand up comedian who resides in Las Vegas, Nevada. Allen has been working in town since 1973. He is also very interested in the spirits who come back to visit us here in the real world. The natural progression for Robert was to put together a company that conducts tours of haunted places in Las Vegas. His Haunted Vegas Tour has turned into a very popular activity for visitors to the city. Originally from Chicago, Illinois, Robert became interested in what he calls "ghost hunting" when he was a child.

"I started out as a musician traveling the road and, as soon as we'd hit a new city, I'd start asking, 'Hey, are any places in this town that are haunted? Are there any hauntings around here?'"

Apparently, Robert never went anywhere without some tools of the trade, including his dowsing rods, which are said to sense ghosts or spirits if they are in an area. The use of these rods has been around for hundreds of years. It is the same type rod that people use to find water when they are planning to dig a well. Most folks who use the rods can't explain exactly how they work, just that they prove very accurate in acknowledging the presence of ghosts or spirits.

Robert provides dowsing rods to all those who go on his tours. For his purposes, they are metal rods bent in an L-shape that the visitors hold in each hand, pointing them toward the area where there might be ghosts. If the rods detect any energy, they cross over each other, signifying that there is something present in the area or room other than the person holding the rods. The silver rods have black coverings on the handle part, and when we (the authors of this book) took the tour, they definitely seemed to have a will of their own, especially when we stopped in one of the spots that we visited. In addition to ghosts, some proponents say you can also find other types of energy and portals to another dimension by using the rods.

"Of course back then everybody thought I was nuts and they called me spooky. Everybody else wanted to go to night clubs; I wanted to go to haunted houses!"

Allen recalls an early experience in his life that proved to him that there might be something to the ghost and spirit stories he had always heard. "My cousin who lived four doors from me, his grandfather died and the house was haunted, and we would go over there and play when I was a kid. We would be on the floor playing toy soldiers and stuff, and the salt and pepper shakers would be going all over the table and stuff would just move, and my aunt would come in and say 'Don't be afraid; it's just grandpa.'

"My cousin's grandfather had died in the bedroom, and all the furniture and everything had been given away, but grandpa never left. So as a kid I was seeing this stuff and I wasn't afraid of it. My whole family was Italian immigrants, but they had all kinds of ghost stories, so I was raised to believe that ghosts aren't going to hurt you, and I've never been around one yet that has. I've been touched, poked, and stroked, but I've never been around one yet that tried to scare me because it didn't want me there. I believe there's a big difference between ghosts and demons, and ghosts don't hurt people because ghosts are people. There may be angry ghosts or cantankerous ghosts, but they don't have the ability to take over your body or hurt you."

We sat down to talk to Robert as we began to research information on stories and legends of ghosts in Las Vegas.

Q: When you came here and got involved in the shows, were you just seeing this stuff or did you experience it?

RA: Certain hotels had ghosts, and as an entertainer, I just was involved in some of it. We were playing at the Plaza Hotel, and one of the stage hands hung himself backstage. I would be in my dressing room and I would hear noises outside that door, and I was the only one down there. My hairbrush would disappear for a few days and then just reappear, and I was the only one with a key to my dressing room. To this day, people who work the Plaza say that the backstage is haunted...they believe he's still there.

Q: What about ghosts at the Hilton Hotel?

RA: Elvis Presley—They've seen his ghost backstage hundreds of times, thousands of times. There was an incident right after he died, where the cleaning lady got on the service elevator and she had towels and all this stuff, and she saw Elvis and spoke to him and then, when she got off the elevator, she realized he had been dead for a year. The Flamingo management brags about Bugsy's (Siegel) ghost, and it's been seen thousands of times.

Q: We've heard your tour is really good.

RA: I try to make it fun because we can't just do a serious ghost tour. Some of the people are very serious, but some just want to go to have a good time, so if you get too serious, you're going to wind up with people snoring or saying they want to leave. We hired comedians to do the tour, not to make light of it because we tell the hauntings legitimately, but you gotta keep people happy. We won't joke about the hauntings, and the same way with the mob tour. We don't joke about the factual stuff, but in between we screw around a lot.

Q: Why do people remain behind as ghosts?

RA: If you look at some of the castles in Scotland, Wales, England, they have ghosts that go back 600 years. Why? Those people were powerful; they didn't want to give up; they had big egos, and I believe a lot of hauntings deal with people's egos. When they die, they don't want to give up what they have or, if they're murdered, they don't want to give up until the murder is solved. They want justice, so there's something that's forcing them or holding them from moving peacefully on to wherever it is we're supposed to go.

And another thing, I call it the loop. A lot of times, ghosts will get hung up trying to finish what they were doing when they died, and they'll do it over and over and over. They're not haunting; they're not there to haunt; they're determined they're gonna finish that job, and they get hung up on kind of a merry go round. You think eventually something would stop them and they would move on, but they don't seem to. Those are my personal opinions, my own theory, because until we die we're never going to be able to prove it. But from what I've seen over the last fifty years, I think that's what it is, just people with very strong personalities or people who've been wronged or people who've been killed at too young an age and don't want to leave. A lot of children are ghosts. You'll hear about some of them on the tour.

Q: What draws people to ghosts?

RA: I don't think most people are drawn to ghosts, I think it's people like us who are interested in it. I think most people are basically afraid of ghosts but they want to confront it because it proves there's an afterlife; because if there are no ghosts, there probably isn't anything else. I mean I think it's just human nature to want to believe in going somewhere versus just going in the ground and that's the end of it. There are people who always stare at accidents, and they'll drive by and look even though it's gruesome. I don't know—there's something about human nature (that) you want to see the dead body. Why do horror films grab so many people? Because people want to sense that fear that goes back to the caveman, where are we going when we die? And I just think that believing in ghosts, looking into ghosts, gives people proof that we're gonna go somewhere, whether it's Heaven, or whatever you believe in.

Q: What can you tell us about the MGM Grand (Bally's) fire?

RA: Well, I stood outside during the original fire; I saw the smoke and just happened to be down there and I watched for hours—you know, from across the street—and there were people jumping and all kinds of weird stuff going on. It started in the kitchen, a loose wire or something, it started smoldering, then it went into the air conditioning system and eventually right into the tower. I mean people were on their balconies because the rooms had filled with smoke, the halls were filled with smoke. They found people in the stairwells overcome with smoke. There were eighty-five people killed in there and some of them are still hanging around the casino—at least that's what this man I know told me. Whenever you have a catastrophe like that, you're gonna have some ghost activity because not everybody's gonna want to move on peacefully.

Q: There are a lot of famous people's ghosts around this town.

RA: Marilyn Monroe's ghost appears in three separate locations, so ghosts can travel. I don't think they're stuck wherever it is they decide to haunt. I used to work in two of the places where she appears.

Q: And you actually knew Liberace...

RA: I knew Liberace and Redd Foxx both. Those guys used to come and see my show after I started playing here in 1973, and I would go see theirs. I mean we weren't best buddies, but I went to Liberace's parties three or four times. I knew him well enough to call him Lee, and he was a nice man. Redd Foxx and I hung out and I played Keno with him a lot of times, and Redd used to tell me, "When I die, I ain't goin' to heaven or hell. I'm coming back here. I want my house back." You see, the IRS had taken his house.

Q: So did he come back?

RA: Oh, his house is extremely haunted. In fact, I just talked to one of my guys who's got the footage of his house being taken by the IRS. That just turned his life around. After that, he turned into a very angry, pistol-packin' old guy, very nasty. Redd was a fun guy until the IRS messed with him. It's his own fault—he never paid taxes, never filed income taxes.

Q: What was Liberace like?

RA: He was a funny guy; he wasn't afraid to laugh at himself; he didn't mind coming out of the closet and letting everybody know it and playing with it. He didn't mind prancing around in silly clothes. He knew they were calling him names, but he didn't care, and it was like he used to say, "Hey, you can call me all the names you want. You paid for all these things." But the real Liberace, when he was not performing, we'd go over to his house, he'd be in the kitchen in his shorts, flipping omelets. He was a tremendous cook. He would have been the next Emeril if he didn't play the piano. He was a warm and nice man.

Q: The Stratosphere is haunted, isn't it?

RA: Oh, yeah. We've had five people jump off the Stratosphere. It is very haunted. You'll hear about that. There are two for sure ghosts, and there are probably more. Bob Stupak was a good friend of mine. I was with him when he designed the Stratosphere on a paper napkin. I worked there for four years, I was the entertainer in Vegas World, and when it switched over to the Stratosphere, I opened for Jerry Lee Lewis; I was his opening act for a year-and-a-half. Bob and I have been friends for thirty years. He got out a blue paper napkin one day in a coffee shop and says, "You ever been to the Eiffel tower?" And I say, "Yeah." He says. "I wanna build this; what do you think?" I asked where, and he said here and I said, "Are you kiddin' me?" He told me he was serious and he was gonna do it. I saw him draw it on a napkin, and then he showed it to me. I told him, "I know you; if you want to do it, you'll do it." It was less than a year later he was starting to build it.

Q: Ghosts, to you, are just a part of everyday activities?

RA: I just accept ghosts as part of a phenomenon that's part of human life. I don't sit around going, "Is it real; is it not real?" I may look at a situation and say, "Is this a real haunting or is it not?" That part of me, the investigator part of me, will look at it that way. As far as my belief in spirits, for me not to believe in ghosts would be to say, "I don't believe in an afterlife; I don't believe in God." My belief system says ghosts exist; therefore, I don't have a problem believing in them, and that doesn't mean that every ghost story I hear, I take as gospel, cause a lot of it is made up. Some of it could be something else, someone thinking it's a ghost, you know, but I've seen enough things in my time, they're just too strange to explain. It's not like some light, and you go, "Well, that could have been something else." I've actually seen things move, I've seen things tumble, I've heard whispering in my ears, I've been touched, I've been stroked and poked, and there was nobody in the room with me, and I'm not imagining it.

I'm a pretty factual person, I don't get hung up in my imagination. I know what I'm feeling and what I'm seeing, and I go into these kinds of things in a detective state of mind. I want it to be phony, I want to find something wrong with it, and then if I can't find something wrong with it, I go, "Well, okay, maybe there's something here." But the tour Haunted Vegas was established primarily as entertainment first, with ghost facts second. When I retired from stand up, I was bored; I wanted to do something, so I started a little ghost tour two nights a week. We had a little van and we went out Friday and Saturday nights. Now we have two buses, we go out every night but Friday, and in October we were doing 90-100 people a night. It grew, I had no idea I was going to do this. I just wanted a hobby.

Q: Can you explain to us about orbs and apparitions?

RA: Well, first you start with an orb. The next step from an orb is ectoplasm, and the next would be a full apparition, but that rarely happens. You very rarely get a full apparition. When you do, you're usually a highly sensitive person, and you'll catch it out of the corner of your eye. It's not like in the movies where you see the ghost walking toward you and he says something. There are people who say they've seen this; I'm not saying that it never happens, but it's a rare thing. In all the years I've been doing this, I've only seen one. It's very rare that you see a full apparition.

31

GLITTER GULCH

Fremont Street, the center of early Las Vegas, is also known as Glitter Gulch, but it wasn't always that way. Because it was the street leading to the train depot, Fremont Street was the center of early downtown Vegas. It was the heart of the business district, with saloons, movie theaters, shops, restaurants (including the first pizza parlor) and gambling halls. Hard as it is to believe now, it also had homes right along the street at that time. It even had the city's first hotel, 1906's Hotel Nevada, and it was Vegas' first paved street (in 1925). In 1931, it boasted the first street light in town and the first gaming license in the state.

Because the street's businesses brightened the night sky with their neon signs and facades, it earned its Glitter Gulch nickname honestly. The most famous sign of all was that of the Pioneer Club's Vegas Vic, the neon cowboy with the moveable arms and a prominent cigarette in those pro-smoking days. Vic spoke ("Howdy, Podner" every fifteen minutes) from the sign's creation in 1951 to the night in 1966 when actors Lee Marvin and Woody Strode shot it with bows and arrows to quiet the sign so they could sleep. After that evening, Vic was forever silent. With a few adjustments over the decades, Vic is still a huge reminder, along with the famed Golden Nugget (the first building in the city designed solely as a casino though it was later remodeled completely by hotel mogul Steve Wynn) of Glitter Gulch's days of dominance in Vegas.

The Fremont Street Experience. *Photo by Liz Cavanaugh.*

The biggest thing here these days, though, is the Fremont Street Experience, a five-block city park pedestrian mall with free concerts and nightly Viva Vision light and laser shows on its canopy displaying over 12 million LED lights that opened in 1995. It also is the site of the Neon Museum, which has restored and displayed the original neon signs of many of the now closed famous hotel-casinos, including the Hacienda and Aladdin Hotels. The Fremont Street Experience's $100 million Neonopolis complex is home to the Poker Dome Challenge, a fourteen-screen movie theater, restaurant, entertainment area, and shops.

Though the Strip has taken over as the face of Vegas, Fremont Street will always be remembered fondly as a major force in and witness to some of the most important moments in the city's history.

32

LAS VEGAS ACADEMY

The Las Vegas Academy of International Studies, Performing and Visual Arts is located in downtown Las Vegas on South Seventh Street. It's considered to be one of the most prestigious arts schools in the country. Students go through a lengthy audition process and must have already selected a major focusing on performing arts, visual arts, or foreign language. While there have been no reports of the school being haunted, a few students would swear that not everyone on the campus is a current student.

Built in 1930, the original campus had only three buildings and was then named Las Vegas High School. This was the first high school in Las Vegas. The location caused a small controversy at first because it involved a long commute for most of the students and its faculty. Still, the school remained open until the late eighties. In 1993, the building became the new home of the Las Vegas Academy of International Studies, Performing, and Visual Arts.

As a high school and performing arts magnet school, several noteworthy students, including many Nevada politicians, have graced the halls over the years. Most notable is singer/actress/choreographer Toni Basil. Born and raised in Las Vegas, Basil was bitten by the show business bug early. Her father, Louis Basil, was the bandleader at the Sahara Hotel and Casino, her mother was part of an acrobatic troupe, Well and The Four Fays. Interestingly, her mother's group performed on the *Ed Sullivan Show* the same night that the Beatles made their famed appearance in February of 1964. Most famous for her 1982 hit "Mickey," Basil was once a cheerleader at Las Vegas High School. Some may remember how she proudly displayed the letters LVHS on the red and white sweater she wore in the song's video. In 2003, Basil's "Mickey" was ranked at number five on VH1's list of the Greatest 100 One Hit Wonders.

Could the ghost of "Mickey" be haunting the halls of Las Vegas Academy? It's doubtful. The song, originally titled "Kitty," was changed to "Mickey" by Basil in honor of her fondness for Mickey Dolenz, the quirky drummer for the sixties band, The Monkees. Dolenz, at last check, is very much alive, not likely to be haunting the building at this time. Maybe later though!

Still, for years students have reported hearing strange sounds in the buildings and have seen the apparition of an old man around campus. The best explanation is that it's the ghost of a gentleman who lived on the property before it became an establishment of higher learning.

Las Vegas High School is now a historical landmark in Las Vegas. The interior of the building has changed, but the exterior remains virtually untouched. Perhaps the gentleman seen around campus is there to finish his education; as they say, you're never too old to learn.

33

EDUCATED GHOSTS

There are several schools located within the city limits of Las Vegas that have reported supernatural goings on.

One school boasting its own unique ghost is the Dell H. Robinson Middle School on Marion Drive where the apparition of an older man walking down the hallways is a common sight. Students report that the man is always dressed as a janitor and walks around with his hands covered in blood. Some students go as far as saying the janitor has followed them home and haunted them in their dreams. The story goes that this only happens to students who are new to the school and will stop happening the first time the student goes to church after the janitor initially makes his presence known.

The Little Blue Choo Choo Day Care Center (3335 Wynn Road) was once a happy place that was filled with toys, books, stuffed bears, and a wonderful train, but it also seems to have had its share of bad luck.

The daycare is now closed because a little boy was killed after being dragged underneath the tracks of the toy train. As if that wasn't bad enough, shortly thereafter, a teacher at the school committed suicide.

Since the Little Blue Choo Choo Day Care has closed, reports claim that on some nights, and occasionally during the day, you can see the image of a little boy digging in the ground with his shovel. Nobody knows who he is, but he seems to appear out of nowhere. Other people have reported seeing the figure of a tiny black woman appear and quickly disappear back into thin air. The daycare building has now been torn down and replaced with another business. Are the small black lady and the young boy still haunting that area or have they moved on? If one hears digging noises when you walk by, the little boy could still be digging his holes in the ground.

Located at 4551 Diamond Head Drive is Edwards Elementary School. Reports from various people claim that a young girl dressed all in white follows students and teachers around. Strangely, the young girl is only visible to fourth grade teachers and students. She seems to appear out of nowhere and is only seen in classroom 26 and in the computer room. Supposedly, the ghost is that of a fourth grader who died while attending the school back in 1990. In a twist similar to the student's claims at the Robinson Middle School, some kids swear that they've seen the young girl in their dreams and allege she haunts them until they share their story with another student.

Interestingly, the Edwards Elementary School's motto is: Discovering Possibilities.

34

THE HAUNTED MANSION THAT NOBODY WANTS

ometimes houses emit a bad aura, and no one knows why. It doesn't have to be an old, dilapidated house that looks like your typical haunted home with crooked shutters and curtains fluttering in the breeze through broken windows. A house that is haunted can look like a regular home—but there's nothing regular about it once you step inside.

Such is the case of a huge mansion located near Wayne Newton's fifty-two-acre ranch, named Casa de Shenandoah for his home state of Virginia. Newton lives at the ranch with his wife, Kathleen, and their daughter, Lauren Ashley. Wayne is known as "Mr. Las Vegas." He's been performing at showrooms in Sin City since the late 1950s, and consistently sells out every show.

Not too far from the entertainer's estate is a beautiful home that has had numerous owners over the years. The original street address for the home was 6660 South Pecos Road. One owner finally had the official street address changed to 6690 South Pecos Road, but once rumors get started, they are hard to cover up. In looking at the house, a new person to Las Vegas might wonder what all the fuss is about. In truth, it could be said of the structure that real estate agents can't give it away because of the stories, truth or fiction, which circulate about it.

According to numerous sources, the house has been bought and sold many times. Legend has it that a horrendous murder was committed in the house soon after it was built. As if the mark of the devil isn't bad enough for a street address, there are also tales of ghosts that roam freely in the home. The story is that even if the house sells, the new owner doesn't live there very long. They may try to refurbish into their own style and personality, trying desperately to ignore all the things they've heard about their new home. Eventually, they all leave.

Realtors talk about the upstairs and how they feel a heavy pressure when they take potential buyers up there. They even go so far as to say there's a feeling of evil about it. People driving by or jogging along the street report seeing a light moving from room to room in front of the windows upstairs. Another account says the figure of a young woman, around the age of sixteen, can be seen going from window to window in the upstairs part of the house. She was supposedly murdered there and, after she was reported missing, police found her body in the house. One man who was on a tour of the home said he felt like he was being pushed into the wall. He got scared and had to leave the building.

Other stories claim the house was the location for a meth lab where drug deals went down. Some even say the dealer was a Satan worshiper, making the house weirder with every tale. Police did raid the house and found a meth lab there. The men who set up the lab hadn't even bothered to buy the building. What with all the ghost tales, they probably figured no one was going to be buying it anytime soon, so they might as well use it for their purposes. What better place to hide an illegal business than a home no one wants?

The current owners will, of course, not let anyone go in the house to check it out unless they seem truly interested in purchasing the mansion. They have asked the tour buses to quit stopping in front of the house.

The haunted house is not a hard place to find, once you figure out where the Newton ranch is at 6730 South Pecos Road. Just drive slowly down the street and look for a gorgeous house that is obviously empty, and you will have found one of Las Vegas' most notorious properties. Remember, though, that this is private property, so please don't trespass.

35

GREEN VALLEY PARK IN HENDERSON, NEVADA, HOSTS GHOSTS

G reen Valley Park in Henderson, Nevada, just outside Las Vegas, is a pretty little green space at the corner of Pecos Road and Millcroft Drive. Children come into the park to play, and families sometimes bring picnic baskets to eat at the tables. An occasional family will grill out at the built-in barbecue pit on the premises. The park offers a piece of solitude in the midst of a town that never turns off its neon lights and where people who play the slots never sleep.

The unsuspecting families who visit the park might be surprised to learn that there are others in the area who never sleep, for the park is reputed to be haunted. The ghosts range from a pioneer woman who was there more than a century ago to a man killed in the area in just the last few years.

The pioneer woman whose ghost resides in the park is the lone survivor from her family, who were following the Union Pacific Railroad tracks west. They were traveling through the region headed to California. They made the unfortunate decision to camp in the area of the present-day park. After pulling their covered wagon into what looked like a safe place, the husband built a campsite where the wife could cook the evening meal for her family, which included several children. After they had eaten their fill, the family bedded down for the night, expecting to be up early the next morning to continue their journey. While they were sleeping, Indians came by, saw the wagon, and investigated the campsite. The natives then killed the husband and children.

The story goes that the wife escaped by jumping in the wagon or a big wooden barrel. This was discovered after some folks from a paranormal group came and investigated the site. There's no word on how the wife died, but she has been seen sitting on the picnic bench, crying over the loss of her husband and children. She is never seen anywhere else in the park, and anyone who has ever seen her reports that she is always sobbing tears of sorrow for her family. Because there were no records kept from that time, no one knows her name or the name of anyone else in her group.

In the 1970s, there were other murders in the park. The bodies of two boys who had been killed were found near the grill by the picnic table. It is believed that the children were around the ages of nine and thirteen when they were killed. Apparently brothers, the court has sealed the records surrounding the case, and very little is known about them, their killer or killers, and how the murder was committed. The family of the children has asked that people not try to contact them or seek to disturb their spirits in the park. People report paranormal activity near the picnic tables and barbecue grill in the park, and visitors who have taken pictures there have had orbs show up in those photos. There is also a photo on the website of one of Las Vegas' ghost tours, Haunted Las Vegas, which shows a couple of orbs around the area. The website is www.hauntedlasvegas.com.

Robert Allen, who owns Haunted Las Vegas tours, says people who take the tour capture images of orbs and streaks at the park all the time. He recalls an incident where a woman on the tour became very adamant that she could see something by the barbecue grill, despite the fact that no one else in the group saw anything. Allen suggested that she take a picture in the direction of where she saw the images. After she had her film developed, she sent Allen an eight-by-ten photograph that clearly showed two ghosts standing by the grill. It is believed they were the images of the boys who were killed in the park, because their bodies were found by that same grill.

Another ghost that haunts the park is that of a 29-year-old man who was killed on November 21, 2004, while trying to cross nearby Interstate 15 on foot. Christopher D. Brown was hit by a car traveling down the freeway, not murdered, so it's possible that the accident happened so quickly that the man doesn't realize he is dead. Since he lived in Henderson and was killed in the vicinity of the park, it is possible that he lives in the park waiting to go on with his life. Brown was the 100th death from a traffic fatality in Nevada that year.

Another park, Fox Ridge in Henderson, is said to be haunted by the ghost of a young boy. The youngster was supposedly killed by a drunk driver near the park. People have reported seeing a swing there moving with no one on it and no wind to cause it to move. They say if you see an apparition and look directly at it, the face turns into a demon and the ghost disappears. Others report that a woman killed by an axe sometimes can be seen in the park.

Green Valley Park is located at 370 North Pecos in Henderson, Nevada. The cross street is Mill Croft. Fox Ridge Park is located at 420 Valle Verde Road in Henderson. The cross street is Fox Ridge. Both are open for visitors to investigate during the day.

Orb floats above the picnic table where two boys were found murdered.
Photo by Liz Cavanaugh.

Another view of Green
Valley Park.
Photo by Liz Cavanaugh.

Giant orb floats above
the grill in the park.
Photo by Liz Cavanaugh.

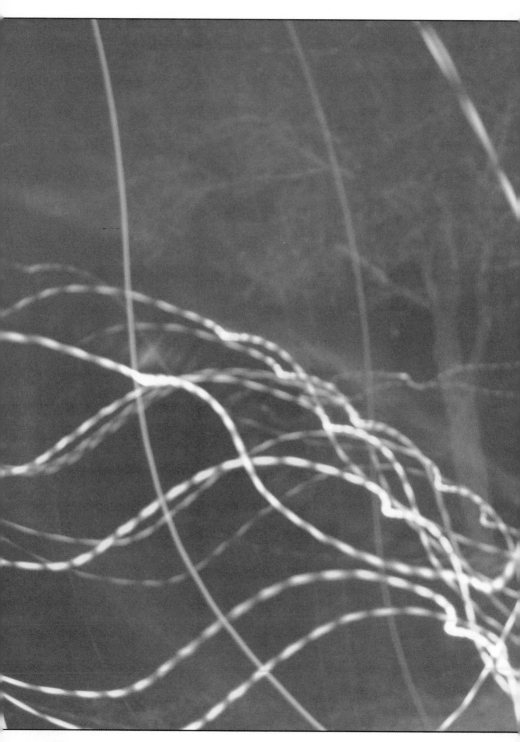

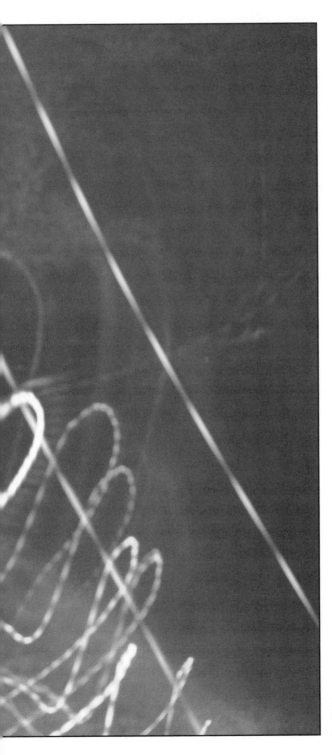

Dancing energy rays at
Green Valley Park.
Photo by Liz Cavanaugh.

36

POTOSI BECOMES NEVADA'S FIRST GHOST TOWN

P otosi, Nevada, has the distinction of being Nevada's first ghost town. Today there are no residents of the settlement and no recorded history of ghosts from its earlier settlers.

Mormons settled in the area to mine lead in 1956. Nathanial Jones, who came there from Salt Lake City, named the town after his boyhood home in Wisconsin. After investigating the mine, he went back to Salt Lake City for supplies, returning to Nevada and establishing a small settlement in December of that year.

The Mormons intended to extract lead to make bullets. A year later, the mine was abandoned, making it the first abandoned mine in Nevada. The reason the Mormons left it was that the ore was too brittle for to use for their original intent, bullets, because it had high zinc content in it.

In 1861, the Colorado Mining Company opened a silver mine in Potosi. At that time, the actual township was laid out and became home to about 1,000 people. There were two short-lived newspapers, J.A. Talbott's handwritten newspaper, *East of the Nevada* or *The Miner's Voice From The Colorado* and the *Potosi Nix Cum Rouscht*.

Around 1870, the Silver State Mining Company tried its hand at mining in the area, renaming the village Crystal City. In the early 1900s, after the Salt Lake and San Pedro Railroad came through the area, the mine was very active. It was purchased by the Empire Zinc Company, which ran it for four years. During that time it became the largest producer of zinc in Nevada. It remained active during World War I, as it was a major source of zinc, lead, and silver.

Potosi is located thirty miles southeast of Las Vegas.

37

AMARGOSA OPERA HOUSE & HOTEL HOME TO MUSIC AND GHOSTS

Death Valley Junction, Nevada, originated as a tent city and grew to become the company town of the Pacific Coast Borax Company. From 1923-1925, the town, comprised of mostly adobe buildings, was home to offices, stores, a dormitory, a hotel, and a recreation venue known as Corkhill Hall. The valley itself has the lowest elevation in North America, sitting at 282 feet below sea level.

The town was located at the junction where the Tonopah and Tidewater Railroads met. It brought transportation to the area so the Pacific Coast Borax Company could ship out product from the borax mines they owned. In 1927, the company moved its facilities closer to a new mine near Los Angeles. Tourists came to the town until the Depression, then the population of Death Valley Junction began to drop. After the construction of the Death Valley National Monument, business picked up once again. Although the railroad ceased to operate, the baby gauge railroad running from New Ryan into two local mines, the Widow Maker and Charley McCarthy, operated so tourists could ride them until the end of the 1950s. Parts of those railroads and the commerce they brought to the area continue to stand today, but the town's population is very low. The area continues to be an area for tourists and those who like to visit areas where ghosts are said to reside.

In 1967, Death Valley Junction took on a new resident. That is the year that Marta Beckett and her husband were traveling through the area. Becket hailed from New York City and had been a dancer since she was three. Her father, a newspaper reporter, took her to many of New York's finest events—the opera, the ballet, the theatre, and concerts—and she was very inspired by these outings. Marta took lessons in dance, as well as piano and art.

Marta danced at Radio City Music Hall and on Broadway in *Showboat, A Tree Grows in Brooklyn,* and *A Wonderful Town.* Soon she was creating her own shows, designing her own costumes, and taking them on the road.

Beckett and her husband were in Death Valley, taking a break after an extensive tour, when they had a flat on their trailer. They were told to go to Death Valley Junction to have it fixed. While Marta was walking around the old town, she spied a building known as the Amargosa Hotel. When she went to examine it further, she found that it housed a theatre. The dancer went inside and was instantly in love. When she saw the building she supposedly said, "Peering through the tiny hole, I had the distinct feeling that I was looking at the other half of myself. The building seemed to be saying.....Take me.....do something with me...I offer you life." Marta decided to rent the hotel and pay for repairs to make it into a working theatre. Renaming it the Amargosa Opera House, the dancer opened the facility on February 10, 1968, performing before twelve people. The theatre has had performances on Friday, Saturday, and Monday ever since. Local residents, as well as tourists who have heard of the venue, come to see Marta perform and to see the fabulous artwork she has painted on the walls and ceiling of the structure. The paintings include murals of audiences, a dancing lady, gypsies, a group of children watched over by their governess, and American Indians. One of the celebrity guests at the Opera House was Red Skelton, who visited there four times after it opened.

Marta's husband left in 1983, but she continues to perform and maintain the Opera House with the help of Thomas J. Willett, who acts as stage manager and emcee of the venue. He also co-stars with Marta in her plays.

Amargosa Opera House, Inc. bought the town of Death Valley Junction. On December 10, 1981, the town of Death Valley Junction was listed in the National Register of Historic Places. It also could be listed on a register of famous ghosts, as the hotel is host to several entities that have been featured on national television. Illusionist Criss Angel did an episode of his show, *MindFreak*, from the Amargosa in 2006. He took in a paranormal group from Arkansas as well as celebrities including singer/songwriter Deborah Gibson, actor Steve Valentine, and the music group Three Six Mafia. One of the people working with the paranormal group was Erin Pavlina, who never had been involved in such an adventure before. She was the woman everyone thought would help communicate with any spirits or ghosts that were in the hotel. Apparently, Criss Angel wanted to confirm the existence of the spirits before he held a séance in the hotel.

Pavlina, who lives in Las Vegas, says she was four years old when she noticed that she was having premonitions about things. "I was highly sensitive and would often know when a disaster was going to strike, and I also knew what people were thinking," she says. "In my teens, I was more into astral projection and communicating with deceased relatives, mostly in my dreams. At that time, I was too afraid to see a ghost in my room. At the time, all this was very scary to me."

During college, Pavlina decided to turn the whole psychic thing off, and it wasn't until she was in her thirties that she watched the television show *Ghost Whisperer* and realized she didn't have to be afraid of her abilities.

"I also found that because I was older and more mature, the vibrations were higher, but were more in a state of love, peace, and harmony, The bad stuff was not able to impact me, and I wasn't fearful, panicked, and anxious like I had been when I was younger. I had learned to keep my energy high and didn't have anything to fear."

It was during this time that Erin discovered she could communicate on the behalf of other people and help them talk to those who had passed on. It was also during this time that she was contacted to be part of the Criss Angel television taping at the Amargosa Hotel.

When they first arrived at the hotel, the group Erin was with encouraged each individual to walk around the building by themselves to find out what vibes they got.

"I was worried, because my guides had told me that I would see something that would be scary to me," Erin says. "I also knew that if I blocked out those experiences, then I would be blocking out the good stuff. I knew I had to go in and be open to whatever experience I had or I would inadvertently block the whole thing.

"The producer didn't tell us what to expect because they wanted honest reactions. They did say we would go into a closed-down portion of the hotel hadn't been used in decades, and advised us to wear simple clothes and close-toed shoes."

Erin says she really didn't want to know much about the place before she had a chance to experience it because she wanted an honest experience there. Even though they weren't briefed, Erin says apparently they felt spirits in the rooms where the crew knew them to be. "They had us go through every room, and we remarked on the energy in each hotel room. Apparently the ones (where) we felt lingering energy were the ones that the owner had mentioned had issues. So really there were three areas we were investigating; one was the theatre, one was the room with baby crying, and the other was this dark unused area where workers used to live."

The hotel was haunted by several ghosts. At one time, someone had committed suicide or murder in the unused area where the crew took the paranormal experts. It is also rumored that a little girl named Mary was murdered in room 34, and people have reported seeing a tall figure at the window, which they think might be the murderer. These same people report an uncomfortable feeling as they walk in to the room 34. A similar feeling is felt when entering the theatre, where another ghost supposedly resides.

One of the reasons the paranormal team wanted Erin along was they thought she might be able to interpret any communication with the entities that were in the hotel. They could record EVP readings, but they would not be able to hear them right away. This was the first time Erin had done this type of thing, but she said it was an amazing experience for her to hear the voices of the spirits and then have what she heard confirmed later by the team's equipment.

"When we went into the theatre, the team was wandering all over the place with their recording devices, but I kept getting a sense there was presence in this one chair. When I told them to go to that chair, they got the spike on the EMF equipment. Later, we found out that was the chair that Marta Beckett's partner used to sit for every performance, and he supposedly died there in the theatre. At the time, I didn't know why we were in theatre. I just sensed the presence in that chair. So that was an interesting combination of my skills and their equipment."

The other thing that happened in the theatre was it was the first place where Erin could actually hear the spirit of Tom answer the paranormal team's questions. "I was actually not being filmed; I was just drinking my water while they were wandering around, asking questions into the air. The first thing I noticed was that when they asked questions I was hearing answers in my mind. I knew I could hear the deceased, but I really didn't expect it. When the pattern became evident to me, I began tuning in more clairvoyantly. I don't see with my eyes but the mind's eye. That was when my attention kept being drawn to that chair. I felt someone was calling to me—this energy was trying to get my attention, and it kept landing on my chair. At that point, I didn't know who it was or what he was about. When they went over with the equipment and got a spike there, we did questions and answers, with them asking the questions and me telling them the responses that I heard."

After they had the experience in the theatre with Erin hearing answers, the team decided to go to the room where people reported hearing a baby crying. "We went over there to see if I could communicate with the baby. I was able to do that, but the baby's energy was a lot different than the adult energy of the guy in the theatre. It had a sense of being lost and alone and afraid, but not a lot of background info because it might not have known its background." Erin says there was a sense of sadness in the room, and she got the distinct impression that the baby did not understand that it needed to cross over.

The unused part of the hotel where Erin and the team went was an old mine shaft where workers for the Borax mine company lived. The area was called Spooky Hollow, and Erin says that is an apt description. She said she and other team members had an overwhelming sensation to get out of the area while they were there. There had been an incident of murder or suicide. "I remember there were spirits talking to me in my right ear, and the team snapped a photo of me and found that an orb was hovering over my ear. This orb was different. It had more of a 3-D

Two orbs float near psychic Erin Pavlina's ear at the Amargosa Opera House. *Courtesy of the Northwestern Arkansas Ghost Connection.*

appearance and it was casting a shadow. I felt it was a different kind of orb. While we were down there, I was in touch with two entities and there were two orbs by my ear in the photograph."

Other members of the team felt weird vibes in two other rooms in the hotel, 33 and 34. It is believed that someone died in room 34. When Erin went in these two areas, she became spooked while the team was asking questions. She says when the spirits were asked who they were, she got the distinct reply, "We are," in a very breathy voice that she describes as demonic. "I called in my spirit guides and told the team that I would say what they were saying but I wouldn't channel them," Erin recalls. She says one of the spirits was a bully who delighted in scaring people. She also remembers that the energy of some of the team members was being pulled out of them. Erin says she was fine the entire time they were in the rooms, and she believes it was because she called in extra spirit guides to help her through that experience.

Erin says it was exciting to identify the entities that others had reported in the hotel. She says the team had never worked with someone like her before so they were amazed at how the sessions turned out. She says she's tried to hook up with other paranormal teams but has not been able to do so.

Criss Angel did conduct a séance at the hotel. He showed about six minutes of footage with the paranormal investigators going around the building and their experiences, and then he did a portion of the show about the actual séance. The show originally aired Halloween night, October 31, 2006. Erin says there was a lot of footage that was not used that might show up on another program in the future.

For those who want to visit Marta and see her play—and check out the other-worldly activities at the Amargosa Hotel—Death Valley Junction is located about ninety-two miles, or a two-hour drive, from Las Vegas on the California border.

38

PIONEER SALOON HAS BULLET HOLES AND GHOSTS

I f Joseph Good's cattle had not liked the water from a spring that flowed near the Spring Mountains, Good might never have discovered silver in the area of the present day town of Goodsprings, Nevada.

The town was named after a Mr. Joseph Good who headquartered his cattle raising operation there. At first, the site was known as Good's Springs, but eventually was called Goodsprings. It was a mining camp with a hotel, a saloon that is still standing and in operation, and a general store. The end of World War I also saw the end of Goodsprings as a mining town. The Keystone gold mine was discovered in 1892, bringing 200 people to the area where Good found silver in 1861. Before the mining era was over, thirty-one million dollars would be made from the lead, gold, copper, silver, and zinc that were mined in the area.

By 1900, a small community had formed made up of tent homes, a mill, and a post office. A school was built in 1913 and is now on the National Register of Historic Places. That was the same year that one of Goodsprings' most famous buildings, the Pioneer Saloon, was built by businessman George Fayle. It remains as the oldest working saloon in Nevada.

The Saloon has several distinguishing features. Its patterned tin exterior and interior walls are thought to be among the last of their kind in the U.S., making the saloon one of the oldest stamped-metal buildings still standing. It is believed that the stamped tin was made by Sears and Roebuck. It has a white-washed appearance that is made to look like stone blocks. Interior squares look the same except they also have a floral design stamped on them.

The cherrywood bar on the premises was supposed to be three times bigger than it is. Manufactured by the Brunswick Company in Maine in the 1860s, the structure was shipped in three sections. Its journey took it around Cape Horn, South Africa and into San Francisco. On its way from Maine to Nevada, one piece was burned in a fire and a second section just never showed up. The third was installed in the saloon in 1913. The pot-belly stove that continues to heat the saloon reportedly dates back to Civil War days.

The saloon was the main focal point in the town during the heyday of the mining era, which slowed down after World War I and finally reached a population of a mere 200 after World War II.

The saloon had its moments in history but in 1954 it closed its doors. Six years later, Irene Nutman opened it again, keeping it for six years before she sold it to Don Hedrick, Sr.

The Hedrick family sold it to Las Vegas entrepreneur Noel Schckells, who thinks the saloon and its history should be preserved. He purchased the building in 2006 for one million dollars and continues to run it today. Visitors to the building will find its history well preserved on its walls, as well as a few ghosts to welcome them as they whet their whistle at the cherrywood bar. Schckells invites travelers and ghosts alike into his saloon with two signs: "Open Everyday 'Till The Drinking Stops" and "Poker Players and Loose Women are Permitted In This Establishment."

Among the more famous of the stories is how actor Clark Gable made the bar his vantage point while he waited for news about his wife, Carole Lombard. The actress was in an airplane that crashed on Mount Potosi not far from Goodsprings in 1942. Twenty-two people lost their lives in the flight, including Lombard and her mother. It is said that you can still see the holes burned by Gable's cigarettes on the top of the bar as he let them slip from his fingers while he numbly waited for three days before finding out that she was dead. Some locals will tell you that Lombard's ghost continues to haunt the saloon, trying to console Gable after he was given the sad news. A melted piece of aluminum, said to have been recovered from the site of a airplane crash that occurred in January, 1942, still sits on top of the pot-bellied stove.

If Lombard's spirit remains at the site, she is not alone. Patrons and bartenders alike often report seeing an old prospector sitting at end of the bar in the evening. Another ghost is said to be that of Paul Coski, who was killed when he was caught cheating at cards. The rather large man was said to have loved his whiskey and before his death had the reputation of beating up two men simultaneously. Visitors to the saloon can see the coroner's report on Coski's death hanging on the wall of the establishment. Maybe he likes to check it out, too, because folks say they've seen a ghostly apparition wearing clothes in the style of the old west lurking in the corners of the saloon while glaring at visitors.

Joe Armstrong was a frequent visitor to the bar. He was a miner who also had the reputation for being the town bully. Apparently, he was also not above cheating at cards, and one night he got caught. Although he denied it when his fellow players confronted him, he stood up and ordered the bartender to cash him out. He then threatened the bartender with a beating if he did not do as he said, pronto. As he moved toward the bar, the bartender pulled a gun and shot him. Legend has his body lying in the saloon for ten hours before someone would take him away. Patrons claim to have seen Armstrong in the bar numerous times, no doubt coming back to try to claim that money he won on the day he died.

More than one poker game got a little out-of-hand in the Pioneer Saloon. The bullet holes in the wall of the bar are not from the time Armstrong was killed. Bartenders usually tell customers that the bullet holes found their way there after a friendly poker game got a little unfriendly back a few years ago.

The saloon is also the site of numerous movies, including *The Mexican*, *Miss Congeniality II*, and *Fear and Loathing in Las Vegas*. Country singer Travis Tritt's cover for his 2004 album, *My Honky Tonk History,* pictures him leaning against the bar.

The Pioneer Saloon, located on West Spring Street, is open every day. It is listed on the Register of Historic Places. Goodsprings is about thirty-five miles from Las Vegas just off I-15 South at the Jean-Goodsprings exit. For information on hours, contact the saloon at (702) 874-9362.

39

ONCE PROMINENT TOWN, RHYOLITE NOW A NEVADA GHOST TOWN

After gold was discovered in the Bull Frog Hills near Death Valley, Nevada, in 1904, it spawned the establishment of a burgeoning settlement. Rhylote is one of the rocks that held the gold found in the area, thus it was a logical choice to name the newly founded town. The Montgomery Shoshone Mine and Mill operated to process the ore. It sold the mine to Charles M. Schwab in 1906.

Rhyolite went on to become of the major cities in the area, at one point housing 10,000 people. It was obvious what was most important to the town's residents, as at one time there were fifty saloons but only eighteen grocery stores.

The new town welcomed electricity in 1907, but production in the mine slowed down beginning in 1908. Despite the fact that the Las Vegas and Tonopah Railroad operated in the town from 1907 to 1914, the town's population was reduced to less than 1,000 people in 1910. By 1911, the mine shut down. Lights and power were turned off in 1916 and in 1919 the post office was closed and the people left to pursue more lucrative jobs elsewhere.

Citizens of Rhyolite thought the town would last forever, as evidenced by the structures that remain. The train depot, which once hosted one of the three railroads that came through town, is still intact. Sitting nearby is a caboose that ran through the town during its heyday. The Cook County Bank building, which cost $90 thousand to build, is now a mere frame of its original three-story structure. It was featured in the movies *The Island* and *Six-String Samurai*. Visitors have reported several ghostly apparitions around the empty vault at these ruins.

The walls of the jail are still standing, although its roof has caved in on the building. The entrance to the abandoned mine is still visible.

Rhyolite resident Tom Kelly built the town's most famous house in 1905. The Bottle House, as it was dubbed, is made of 51,000 bottles. It is still standing, and in 1925 it was used in the movie *The Air Mail*, a silent film by Paramount Pictures released in 1926. It starred Warner Baxter, Billie Dove, Millie Brian, and Douglas Fairbanks, Jr. The film could be considered a ghost of itself as well, because there are only four of the original

The Bottle House at Rhyolite. *Photo courtesy of The Bottle House.*

The train station at Rhyolite. *Public Domain—courtesy PDPhoto.org.*

eight reels that remain housed in the Library of Congress in Washington, D.C.

The Bottle House has been fenced off to protect it from vandals and remains one of the more popular sites to photograph in the area. Those folks who stop by to take a photo or two report seeing Kelly's ghost in the house that he built when Rhyolite was a booming metropolis.

Other ghostly figures can be seen at the Goldwell Open Air Museum at the southern entrance to the town off Highway 374. It is here that a group of Belgian artists, led by the late Albert Szukalski, created seven outdoor sculptures. Among them are what has been described as a "ghostly" interpretation of the Last Supper painting by Leonardo Da Vinci. There are other contributions as well, including a twenty-five-foot high pink woman made of cinder blocks and a twenty-four-foot high steel prospector accompanied by a penguin. Obviously, the painters were not too concerned with making the sculptures totally true to life to the area! The park is open to visitors every day. Rhyolite is located about eighty-five miles northwest of Las Vegas off U.S. Highway 95 on Highway 374.

40

GOLDFIELD HOTEL HOST TO NUMEROUS GHOSTLY GUESTS

T he ghost town of Goldfield, Nevada, was at one time the largest city in the state. When it was in the midst of its gold mining boom, the city had a population of 35,000, which supported three newspapers, five banks, and numerous hotels, restaurants, and saloons.

Among those hotels was the Goldfield, which was often cited as the most opulent hotel between Chicago and San Francisco. Today, the building, though currently closed and under renovation, boasts a number of ghostly apparitions that live within its walls.

The hotel was designed by architect George Holesworth and opened in 1908. Its first owners were a group of investors that included J. Franklin Douglas. Though it cost just over $300 thousand to build, the hotel had 154 heated rooms with electric lights. Mahogany graced the lobby walls, and the check-in area was also made of mahogany. There was gold-leaf on the ceilings, from which hung crystal chandeliers. Leather upholstery made the lobby a very luxurious place to relax while waiting for someone to come down from their room in the first Otis elevator to be installed west of the Mississippi. The owners hired chefs from Europe to cater to every whim of the elite in society who could afford to stay at the luxury lodging.

George Wingfield, owner of the Goldfield Consolidated Mines Company, and Casey McDannell bought the business soon after it opened. It was merged into a company called the Bonanza Hotel Company, which owned several other hotel properties. Wingfield went on to become a prominent politician in Nevada, owning banks, ranches, and other hotels.

The hotel sold a third time, in 1923, to Newton Crumley, who also owned other hotels. Crumley wanted to capitalize on the gold in the area in order to make even more money, so he dug two mine shafts under the hotel two years later, but neither yielded any gold for him. As the mining era of the town ended, so the hotel began to decline as well. By the 1930s, it had lost most of its grandeur and was home to a much less genteel clientele. While World War II was going on, the structure was home to Army Air Corp personnel who were assigned to Tonopah Air Base near the town. In 1945, the hotel permanently closed.

When most of the gold had been mined, somewhere around 1920, the town dropped in population to around 1,500 people. In 1923, a fire swept through the town, eliminating 27 blocks of homes and businesses. Currently, less than 500 people live in Goldfield, not counting the hotel's current residents.

Since that time the hotel has been in great disrepair. The structure is still sound, and several people have sought to buy it and restore it to its original state. In 1985, a man named Lester O'Shea did begin restoration, but the company he owned went bankrupt after it was about eighty-five percent complete and the project was never finished. As recently as 2003, Edgar "Red" Roberts bought the property at auction with plans to complete the restoration that was begun twenty years earlier. He hopes to have forty guest rooms, a casino, and a café.

Even though the Goldfield is not presently open for business, it seems that some previous residents continue to haunt the establishment. Paranormal experts have declared that the hotel is one of seven doorways that can be found on this planet for spirits to enter and leave the different dimensions. This philosophy is based on ley lines, which are hypothetical alignments of a number of places of geographical interest, such as ancient monuments and megaliths.

As many as a dozen spirits have been seen in the structure. In the past, many experts have visited the hotel and recorded photos of orbs and ghosts as well as audio of what is believed to be voices (EVP) of the spirits. One person who calls herself Amandaquerque gives a full account of two nights she visited there in 2008 at the website www. squidoo.com. She was at the hotel with a crew of people from the Ghost Adventure called the Ghost Posse.

The first night, she roamed the hotel at will with very little happening except that she was creeped out and didn't go into a couple areas of the building. One was the mine shaft room, the other a hallway on the fourth floor of the hotel.

On the second night, when the entire group explored the hotel together and recorded the visit, things were a little more exciting. Amandaquerque says the basement was very cold, enough for them to see their breath in the air. They could feel a presence and one of the crew members thought someone was pulling her hair. In room 109 they were able to record a voice saying the same thing on two different recorders—"I'm in the wall."

They also did a session on the third floor where they attempted to record audio. It was there that they saw a shadow figure that moved toward them and remained visible for about ten minutes. When the spirits were asked to show themselves while everyone was sitting in the hallway, Amandaquerque says a small stone sailed through the air from one end of the hallway to where they were sitting. When asked to do it again, the spirit obliged them. The crew had some problems with the cameras during this part of the evening.

While Amandaquerque doesn't identify the various ghosts they encountered, several of them have been identified over the years. One is supposedly the owner of the mine that was first on the site, who haunts the second floor. Two spirits are thought to be those of two people who committed suicide in the hotel. The woman hung herself, and the man, described as elderly, jumped out a window on one of the upper floors.

There's also a ghost called "The Stabber" who haunts the Gold Room, which was at one time the main dining room of the hotel. Apparently, no one has ever been able to determine who he is or why he threatens people with a knife.

Children also live within the walls of the hotel. People have reported seeing two children and a smaller figure, thought to be a midget who might have been part of one of the side shows of the numerous carnivals that traveled the area during the hotel's heyday. They are most often seen at the bottom of the staircase on the lobby level of the building, and they have been known to play pranks on visitors.

The most famous ghost will be even more famous if movie producers have their way. Elizabeth, a prostitute who frequented the hotel in its early years, supposedly resides in room 109. As the story goes, Elizabeth became pregnant by one of her frequent clients, hotel owner Wingfield. He was not happy that she was having a baby and supposedly kept her chained in room 109, where she pleaded for mercy until she gave birth, at which time both she and the baby mysteriously disappeared. Still another version of the story says she died in childbirth and the baby was thrown down the old mine shaft under the hotel. It is said that Elizabeth haunts room 109, continually seeking to find the child she lost. Eerie cries from a baby also have been heard in the hotel over the years.

Critiques point out that there are a few discrepancies in the story, but when it comes to ghosts, that only makes it more mysterious. Those who have seen her ghost describe Elizabeth as being dressed in a white or light colored gown with long hair. Visitors often say their cameras work in other areas of the hotel but not in room 109. Animals also refuse to cross the threshold of the permanently cold room. A movie about her, titled *In Canaan's Land*, is currently in pre-production. It can be found listed on the website www.imdp.com.

George Wingfield himself is said to haunt the hotel. Visitors have smelled cigar smoke and even seen fresh ashes in the first floor room where he once lived. They also report seeing him or smelling smoke near the staircase in the lobby. Reports have never put this presence and the apparition of Elizabeth together, though.

The hotel has been featured on several television shows, including Fox Family TV's *World's Scariest Places* in 2001 and the Sci-Fi Channel's *Scariest Places on Earth* in 2008.

Goldfield is located about three hours northwest of Las Vegas on Highway 95.

41

CHEF HAUNTS
FAVORITE RESTAURANT
IN DEATH VALLEY

F urnace Creek Inn & Ranch Resort is a quaint little
sanctuary in the midst of Death Valley, California. The
inn, which opened in 1927, is located on the salt flats of
Death Valley National Park, about two hours from Las Vegas.
The mission-style hotel sits in the midst of scenic mountains
and canyons that encompass a rainbow of colors. It is such a
beautiful area that Hollywood producers have filmed movies
and television shows there.

The adobe bricks that make up the thick walls of the structure
were made by hand by Paiute and Shoshone Indians hired to build
the facility. The thick walls allow temperatures inside to be cool while
outside they have been recorded as high as 125 degrees. To help
alleviate the hot weather, a swimming pool was built at the resort in 1930.
While the area is beautiful, the temperatures were a source of
annoyance to those traveling through the area, prospecting for
gold in the mid-1800s. Men and women hoping to strike it rich
found the region dangerous as they made their way through the
hot desert.

One might suppose that any ghosts haunting the inn and
resort would be miners or other folk who lost their lives seeking

Furnace Creek Inn and Ranch Resort in Death Valley, California,
near Nevada state line.
Courtesy of Furnace Creek Inn and Ranch Resort.

their fortunes in the gold towns of the American West. Not so,
according to local legend—the most famous spirit in the area is
a more modern one who once worked at the restaurant there.

Chef James Marquez was a well-known chef at the Furnace
Creek Inn & Ranch Resort, working in the restaurant's kitchen
from 1959 to 1973. Unfortunately, while the chef worked at
the restaurant at Furnace Creek, he was taken ill and had to
quit his job at the resort. He died three years later, never able
to return to work in his beloved kitchen. Soon after his death,
workers at the restaurant began hearing strange noises during
the night coming from the dining room. They would find
kitchen equipment moved around after they had put it up the
day before. They also heard and saw doors opening and closing
when no one was close to them. Finally it was determined that
Chef Marquez had returned to the kitchen where he once worked
and was overseeing the jobs being done there, as he did when
he was alive. No one has yet decided if he moves things around

to show his disapproval of the new staff, or if he's just trying to be helpful while his spirit resides at his former workplace.

Furnace Creek Inn & Ranch Resort is located on Highway 190 in Death Valley, California. It is about 120 miles northwest of Las Vegas. Another interesting fact about the resort—they boast an eighteen-hole golf course that has the distinction of being the lowest in the world, as it sits 214 feet below sea level. Other amenities include restaurants, a saloon, stores, a Borax Museum, tennis courts, horseback riding, massage therapy, a 3,000-foot airstrip, a service station, and conference and banquet facilities. The Furnace Creek Inn is open from Mid-October through mid-May.

If you wish to check out the resort's famous chef, call (760) 786-2345 for reservations. Interestingly enough, the hotel's website does not mention that a ghost calls Furnace Creek Inn & Ranch Resort home.

42

OATIE THE GHOST WALKS THE STREETS OF OATMAN

The Oatman Hotel, just over the Arizona line in the tiny town of Oatman, is proud of its resident ghost. Oatie, as locals call him, is a spirit who likes to play a few tricks on people at the hotel. He's not discriminatory—he pranks folks who work there as well as overnight guests.

Oatie's real name was William Ray Flour, an Irish immigrant drawn to the area because of the discovery of gold. He lived in the hotel when he first arrived in town and soon sent for his family, a wife and two children. The journey to Arizona from Ireland proved too hard for them, and they died on the way to meet Flour. The miner apparently sank into a deep depression from losing his wife and children and soon became a heavy drinker. The story goes that he drank himself to death in 1930. Legend has it that his body was not found for two days. When it was discovered behind the hotel, he was quickly buried in a shallow grave near the location where the body lay.

Apparently Flour still has not left the premises. Perhaps he is in denial and chooses to continue living at the hotel, awaiting the arrival of his family to join him from his home country. He has been seen or heard in the room where he lived, as well on his favorite bar stool in the hotel's saloon. The establishment rents out the room where Oatie supposedly lives to visitors who are interested in possibly having a ghostly encounter with him. The town claims Oatie, too, as they have a celebration in his honor on St. Patrick's Day.

In 2001, Mike Kepka was staying at the hotel with a friend, Kevin Fagan, a reporter from the *San Francisco Chronicle*, who was there to do a travel piece on Oatman. Kepka chose to stay in the room where Oatie is known to be heard. The next morning Mike reported he got little sleep because he kept hearing someone or something tapping with ghostly fingers on the wall behind the headboard of his bed.

Peg Robertson, owner of the Lasting Impression photo shop in the town, agreed with Mike that the sounds he heard had to be Oatie. She told Fagan that her shop once was in the hotel and, when she first opened it there, she didn't believe Oatie really existed. That opinion changed quickly because Oatie seemingly set out to prove that he was real. Robertson said that she saw a doll in her shop go sailing through the air several times, apparently at the hands of Oatie. At other times, objects in the shop would be moved from where she had last placed them. She hastened to add that she never felt Oatie was a dangerous ghost, just someone who liked to have a little fun. He was also a music lover, as he is known to play the bagpipes at night. He also likes country music and occasionally will spin Merle Haggard's hit song from the 1960s, "Okie from Muskogee," even when the jukebox isn't plugged in!

Oatman was a major mining town in its day. Although there were people in the area beginning around 1906, it wasn't until 1915 when two prospectors found gold in the area that a tent camp became the first official settlement named Vivian for the Vivian Mining Company. Within a year, the city boasted a population of 3,500.

The town was renamed in memory of a family named Oatman, six of whom were killed by the Yavapai Indians who lived in the area. Of the surviving three family members, a daughter, Olive, was traded to the Apache before she was finally rescued near the current town in 1857. Interestingly enough, no one has ever reported seeing the ghosts from anyone in the Oatman family checking out the town named after them.

The hotel, which was built in 1902, was originally called the Durlin Hotel. It has the distinction of being the place where Clark Gable and Carole Lombard chose to spend their wedding night on March 29, 1939. To this day, visitors can stay in the room, which is decorated in a similar style to the original furnishings of the space. Some folks even report they've heard the happy couple whispering and laughing in the room as they pass by.

Other phenomenon have been reported in the Theatre Room Museum and the hotel bar. Footprints appear out of nowhere and outlines of bodies are seen on the beds in the museum. Guests in the saloon report if they lay money on the bar it disappears and their glasses mysteriously move if they don't hold on to them.

Mining operations were shut down in 1941 by the U.S. Government, which deemed it was more important to mine other metals during World War II. Travelers along Route 66 rediscovered Oatman for a few years before the interstate system came along to divert drivers to a faster means of getting around the country.

Today, Oatman is a sleepy little town that welcomes visitors who still enjoy the slow pace of Route 66 and the history of the old west. Burros roam the streets, descendents from those brought to the area by miners in search of gold and other precious metals. Be aware that the four-legged creatures always have the right of way! A lot of Route 66 memorabilia and information, as well as the history of the mines from the area, can be found in shops and museums in the city. The city is a favorite spot for motorcyclists who enjoy the beauty of the surrounding area from their bikes. There are numerous activities in the town, including gunfights in the streets, tours of the old gold mines, and treks through the desert in your choice of Hummers or stagecoaches.

The Oatman Hotel became a museum for awhile but it is no longer open. Visitors can now enjoy the bar and restaurant downstairs and visit the Clark Gable Honeymoon Suite upstairs, where there is also a banquet room available by reservation. Oatman is about 135 miles west of Las Vegas on Route 66. It is located at 181 Main Street. Call for more information: 928-768-4408.

43

CHLORIDE & MINERAL PARK MINING TOWNS HOST GHOSTS

The town of Chloride, located south of Hoover Dam, has maintained the charm that comes from being built the 1800s. The name is derived from ore in which was found silver, lead, zinc, turquoise, and gold. The first people to mine the area were soldiers from Fort Mohave.

From its meager beginnings in 1860, the town grew to around 2,000 residents in 1920, brought in by the Butterfield Stage line from 1868 to 1919 and the Santa Fe Railroad from 1898 to 1935. Early settlers had to deal with the local Hualapai Indians, who at one point stole some of the miner's guns. They killed several of the miners and were a general thorn in the side of the people who were settling the area.

In 1870, the new residents negotiated a peace treaty with the Indians and the settling of the area went much more smoothly. After the cost of mining increased in the 1940s, the mines in the area were shut down and people began moving elsewhere to find other employment. Visitors continued to come there, however, and in the 1960s, a group of hippies settled there. Roy Purcell, who was a part of that group, painted murals on the rocks located above the town close to the old mines.

Among the old buildings that survived several fires in Chloride are the Santa Fe Railroad Station, a two-room jail, a bank vault, and the Chloride post office, which is the oldest continually functioning post office in the state.

Mineral Park is located just six miles south of Chloride. It has a slight shorter history, having been established in 1871, eventually becoming the county seat of Mohave County. The Atlantic & Pacific Railroad ran through the area in 1883. The same railroad that brought them transportation also brought it to nearby Kingman, which grew even more rapidly and eventually became the capitol of the county.

The post office was established in Mineral Park December 31, 1872, and stayed active until June 15, 1912. The town basically became a total ghost town at that point, although there are some reminders of the town that today fall under the protection of a mining company.

While Mineral Park is a real ghost town with no residents, Chloride has maintained its status as a town of around 300 people. They share their space with a few ghosts from the town's history.

Residents and visitors report sighting a dark-skinned woman in one of the buildings on Tennessee Avenue. She has long black hair and has been observed walking around in broad daylight, then disappears. On the same street sits the Mineshaft Market. There was once a movie theatre on the lot next to it, but in the early 1900s the lot was cleared. A bulldozer was attempting to move some large concrete blocks when workers reported hearing groans coming from the vicinity of the dozer.

A few weeks later the owner of the Mineshaft Market was standing on the lot, looking into the sky and observing satellites. He happened to glance toward the end of the lot where he saw a vapor-like image which grew larger as he watched. He then heard moans coming from that apparition. While no one else in Choride has reported seeing a similar sighting, campers who have set up on the lot say they've seen similar images during their stay there.

Other reports from folks say that the mountains behind the town light up at night. Although people have checked the area, there are no lights that would cause this to happen and there are no roads where the headlight of cars shine onto the mountains.

In Mineral Park, mine workers say they've seen a man sitting above them on a cement wall. Middle aged and wearing black pants, a white shirt and a flat brimmed hat, he sits and watches them as they work. If they try to approach him, he disappears, but as soon as they resume work, he reappears. They are not sure if he is a miner from the old mines in the area or perhaps a supervisor from the mines who just wants to make sure the men are all carrying out their proper duties!

Miners on the night shift who have reason to go inside the office building have heard people talking, filing cabinet doors opening and closing, and people walking through the corridors. They have seen people walking around but they vanish when anyone approaches them. Word is that some workers get so spooked by the apparitions and noise that they quit rather than have to return to the building. Other areas of the mine in Mineral Park have strange effects on people, whether they walk through them in daylight or dark. Watchmen report that when they walk through these areas the hair stands up on the back of their neck. Workers also report that they sometimes see a glow rise out of the darkness above the moly a area of the mine.

Visitors are not allowed on the Mineral Park Mine property. Those who wish to visit Chloride and experience its ghostly phenomenon should contact the Chloride Chamber of Commerce at (520) 565-2204.

44

HOOVER DAM AND BOULDER CITY HOTEL HOST GHOSTS OF THE PAST

Hoover Dam, formerly known as Boulder Dam, and the Boulder Dam Hotel have their own interesting tales. The dam attracts over one million visitors each year. Everyone wants to know how many people died while the dam was being built. That story alone has a twist of irony to it.

On December 20, 1922, J.G. Tierney drowned after he fell into the Colorado River from a barge. Tierney was a Bureau of Reclamation employee and was in the area as part of a geological survey. The group he was with was seeking to find the ideal spot to build Hoover Dam. They ended up building in the same area where the accident occurred.

Thirteen years later, on December 20, 1935, Patrick W. Tierney died at Hoover Dam. He fell from an intake tower and was killed. Patrick was the son of the aforementioned J.G. Tierney. Legend has it that they were the first and last men to lose their lives in conjunction with the building of the dam.

All told, 112 people died in that 13-year time period. Another surveyor also died in conjunction with the dam, but he

A beautiful shot of the great Hoover Dam. *Public Domain—courtesy PDPhoto.org.*

was not in the area where the dam was eventually built. Harold Connelly died on May 15, 1922, when he fell off a barge and drowned in a canyon located upstream from where the dam is today.

There have also been suicide attempts at the dam. Eventually people were no longer allowed to go to the top of the dam because so many people went there to try to jump to their death in the rushing waters below. Perhaps these account for people's stories about seeing the ghosts of people in the waters beneath the dam.

It is said that a worker killed in the 1930s actually haunts the dam. People have seen him where the generators are located, hoping to make contact with the real world. Another man who died in 1983, after slipping and falling over the railing, also haunts the premises. This ghost continues to walk around the facility to ensure that things are running as they should. Others have heard someone calling to them in the elevator. It is not sure if these last two entities are the same person.

Boulder Dam Hotel. *Public Domain—courtesy PDPhoto.org.*

In January 2009, a bus carrying Chinese tourists en route to Las Vegas overturned on US 93 near Hoover Dam. Sixteen people were injured; seven died at the scene.

The nearby Boulder Dam Hotel in Boulder City also has an interesting history. It was built in 1933, originally to house the workers who would build the dam. The owners thought it would become a destination resort. Certainly it lived up to its expectations as visitors from the U.S., Asia, and Europe flocked to it as they journeyed to the area to see the new dam. Celebrities, including Shirley Temple, Will Rogers, and Bette Davis, booked rooms there. Even Howard Hughes stayed at the hotel after wrecking his Sikorsky-S43 at nearby Lake Mead. On July 13, 1982, the hotel was named to the National Register of Historic Places.

Visitors have reported they hear a person singing and also the sounds of a piano. Others have reported doors that open and close, a smell of cigarette smoke when no one in the room is smoking, and other strange noises and ghostly sightings.

Some have reported seeing spirits float by them and feeling a presence in the room with them. Visitors to the hotel also report feeling a presence in the Tiffany Restaurant in the hotel. There are also rumors of a worker who was killed and buried in the basement. Some have reported seeing his ghost in the basement of the hotel.

The hotel closed in 1941, then reopened in 1945 after the end of World War II. Shortly thereafter, one of the investors in the Boulder Dam Hotel was found dead in the Colorado River, his pockets heavy with rocks. Authorities ruled his death a suicide. In the 1960s, the hotel was used as a rest home for the elderly.

When there was real danger that the building might be torn down, several groups came together to save it. The Boulder City Arts Council, Chamber of Commerce, Museum and Historical Association, and the city bought the building in 1993. The renovations they have made have been as much in keeping with its original style as possible. More than two million dollars was spent on renovations. The hotel is now open daily for business.

The book *Midnight on Arizona Street* records the history of the hotel and talks about the ghosts that are found within its walls.

The Boulder Dam Hotel Bed and Breakfast, as it's now called, is located at 1305 Arizona Street in Boulder City, Nevada. If you want to check it out, contact the remodeled facility at 702-293-3510.

45

AREA 51: ALIENS AMONG US?

The existence of Area 51 (about 85 miles northwest of Las Vegas) itself may have been declassified in 1997, and officially admitted as operative by the U. S. government in 2003, but there's still enough mystery surrounding it to raise wild speculation by fervent conspiracy theorists and UFOers.

The famous black mailbox, now painted white, near Area 51. *Photo by Liz Cavanaugh.*

Area 51 is located inside a secret military base near Nevada's Groom Lake, and trespassers are subject to arrest or even being shot by tenacious guards. Most often, however, fines (approximately $600 a transgression) and subsequent interrogations/discussions with agents from the FBI are the penalty. Signs posted all over the site's perimeters read, "Photography is prohibited" and "The use of deadly force is authorized." It's also a

no-flyover zone even for most military aircraft, not just civilian planes. Military pilots call its airspace The Box.

Many believe, however, that another kind of aircraft—the extraterrestrial type with alien pilots—is more than welcome to fly over and even land in The Box. For years, it has been rumored that the infamous wrecked flying saucer supposedly taken from Roswell, New Mexico, is still hidden in a building at Area 51.

The area was first used for the Army Air Corps Gunnery School during World War II. It fell into disuse after the war until 1955. The super-secure base, close to the Nevada Test site where atomic weapons were tested for years, is said to have been built and opened then by the CIA alone or in partnership with the Atomic Energy Commission and Lockheed. Reportedly, the U-2 spy plane and Blackbird aircrafts were first tested here. President Eisenhower initially signed the first Executive Order which restricted airspace over Area 51, and all the subsequent presidents have continued to protect the classified information for operations at Area 51. The area now is under the control of the Air Force and the Department of Energy in what seems at first glance to be an odd pairing.

What is known suggests that it is a development, testing, and training site for highly secret experimental aircraft (including the Stealth fighters) and weapons. Of course, a lot of avid UFO believers think much of the technology for these new aircraft comes from captured alien spacecraft that have been kept and studied at Area 51 and from live extraterrestrial beings who supposedly have been meeting through the years with base personnel. Some people even believe

Entering Area 51. *Photo by Liz Cavanaugh.*

Another warning sign, approaching Area 51. *Photo by Liz Cavanaugh.*

that time travel experimentation and weather control development are being worked on at the base.

That may not be all that has been kept under covers at the base. In 1994, the Air Force and U. S. Environmental Protection Agency were sued by ex-workers and the widows of late workers who were supposedly exposed to toxic chemical materials at the base that had caused death in two cases and terrible injuries to the liver, respiration system, and skin of the others. Because President Bill Clinton exempted the base from environmental disclosure laws in a Presidential Determination for national security reasons, there was not enough evidence and the lawsuit was dismissed. Appeals were rejected because revelation of military capabilities would have occurred if information on the materials present in the base's air was disclosed, a menacing fact in and of itself.

Maps of the area don't show Area 51, and satellite maps have it blocked out. Even Skylab astronauts were forbidden to photograph the area from space.

The movie and television world isn't afraid to delve into the possibilities of what might have been taking place in Area 51, which some have termed Dreamland or Paradise Ranch. It was featured in the movies *Independence Day*, *Tomb Raider 3*, and *Indiana Jones and the Kingdom of the Crystal Skull*, as well as the television series *Stargate SG-1*, *Seven Days*, and *Metal Gear*.

Strange alien gift shop near Area 51. *Photo by Liz Cavanaugh.*

Alien being or possible tourist visiting Area 51. *Photo by Liz Cavanaugh.*

The sign says it all. *Photo by Liz Cavanaugh.*

The coolest—or most amusing—clue may be from the government itself, which named a 98-mile section of Route 375 the "Extraterrestrial Highway." That may be the only sign of a sense of humor that the government has shown in any way concerning the most mysterious and controversial air base (if indeed, that is what Area 51 is) in the world.

46

THE LITTLE A 'LE' INN

P art of the fun of exploring the territory around Area 51 is spending some time at a strange little place called the Little A 'Le' Inn, located in Rachel, Nevada. Just a 149-mile drive from Las Vegas, the Little A 'Le' Inn is a place to kick back, do a little Martian hunting, and just take it all in.

After you've visited the Groom Lake Road warning signs, checked out red flag military exercises, and snapped a photo of the "black

Earthlings Welcome. *Photo by Liz Cavanaugh.*

The Little A 'Le' Inn. *Photo by Liz Cavanaugh.*

mailbox," you'll be ready to grab an Alien Burger and sip a cold one. You'll also have a chance to buy souvenirs of little green men and catch up on the latest area gossip with the bartender or others who have come for the exact same reason. It's a great escape from the casinos and the bustle of the Strip.

The drive to Rachel is an easy one and tends to fly by. The bright lights and neon signs of Las Vegas disappear into the desert just a few miles outside the city. An hour or so out of town, you begin to think you could drive forever without seeing another car. Be advised, this isn't a drive you want to do at night. The long stretches of straight, flat road, with just the moon and the stars to light your path, can easily make a person forget there is such a thing as a speed limit. Miles and miles of grazing land sit on either side of the highway. You hit a cow, and you pay; you hit a big cow, and your estate pays. It's also a good idea to keep an eye on your gas tank. It's a good fifty miles from the Little A 'Le' Inn to the nearest filling station.

From the time you turn into the gravel drive, you know you're in alien country, from the old parked tow truck dangling a small spaceship off the back to the graphics of happy, waving aliens, painted on the white buildings. It's the kind of place you could easily speed right past if you weren't looking for it, but the friendly staff and interesting array of guests that it attracts makes you glad you stopped.

For over twenty years, The Little A 'Le' Inn has been welcoming visitors. The walls of the diner/souvenir shop are covered in photos of reported UFO sightings, alien beings, and spaceships. The shelves are full of coffee mugs, t-shirts, ball caps, flying saucer driver's licenses, alien beanie babies, alien head soap-on-a-ropes, and spaceship ashtrays. Brochures, books, and pamphlets are casually strewn around the counters and available to purchase. As for the menu, it's strictly from another world.

Outside, the grounds are full of picnic tables and lawn chairs, a couple of flower beds, places to camp and park your RV, and a few small trailer homes that serve as motel rooms. Be warned, unless you book both guest rooms in a trailer, you'll be sharing the bathroom. UFO enthusiasts gather here several times a year to share information and swap tales.

Haunted trailer accommodations at The Little A 'Le' Inn. *Photo by Liz Cavanaugh.*

All sorts of stories circulate about the strange things seen in the clear skies around Rachel, Nevada. Other stories circulate about the strange things that have happened to guests in the trailers. Especially in rooms two and five.

No one knows if ghosts haunt the property, or if the strange sights and sounds are coming from non-earthly beings just passing through. Guests have been awakened in the middle of the night by the sound of tapping on their windows. Some have reported seeing unusual lights flashing outside their windows, as well as hearing strange sounds. Some guests have simply gotten up, grabbed their stuff, and hit the road, preferring the "safety in numbers" theory, and headed back to a more populated area.

It would be difficult for anyone, not used to such peace and darkness, to try to sleep in the dead quiet of Rachel, Nevada. It's also totally understandable that some folks might feel uneasy after visiting all the nearby sights and hearing the stories about strange spaceships and unknown beings. After all, no one really wants to be abducted by an alien, or kept awake all night thinking about the possibilities!

47

FUN FACTS ABOUT SIN CITY & NEVADA

Two of the most common fun facts about Las Vegas and her home state involve animals. First, it is still illegal to drive a camel on the highway in Nevada. Secondly, it's perfectly legal to hang a person that shoots your dog, as long as your dog is on your property when it bites the bullet.

Did you know that Las Vegas has nearly seventy different religious faiths represented within the city limits? That gives Sin City the largest number of churches per capita in the U.S. Churches routinely find casino chips in their offering plates.

The Entertainment Director at the Tropicana hotel, that brought the famed Follies Bergere to their showroom, was Lou Walters. His daughter is Barbara Walters.

The Dunes was the first hotel to feature topless dancers in their show, Minsky's Follies. This was back in 1957. The hotel had opened two years earlier, but hadn't kicked into high gear until the ladies kicked off their tops.

Footage of the Sands Hotel's implosion was incorporated into the 1996 feature film *Con Air*, starring Nicolas Cage. In the film, a jetliner crashes into a Strip hotel. The implosion worked perfectly as the backdrop for the scene.

Casino chips from many of the hotels which have been torn down or imploded are now collectors' items. Some, such as certain denominations from the Sands, can bring in up to $1,000 each. The best place to find old casino chips is on EBAY. A good site for more information on this hot hobby is: www. newcasinochips.com.

There are no mosquitoes in Las Vegas. Really. The lack of annual rainfall and dry desert air give them very few, if any, places to breed.

The Union Plaza hotel was the first establishment to hire female dealers in their casino.

Boulder City is the only city in Nevada where gambling is illegal. If you're headed to Hoover Dam, you'll pass right through Boulder City.

The first airplane landed in Las Vegas in 1920.

The average Las Vegas Valley household consumes about 230,000 gallons of water a year.

The famous Las Vegas Strip is not located in the city of Las Vegas. The Strip actually comes under the jurisdiction of Clark County.

The all-time single concert box-office record occurred in Las Vegas. The show, starring Barbra Streisand, took place at the MGM Grand on New Year's Eve in 1999. The show grossed $14,694,750 from 12,477 tickets sold.

There is one operating slot machine in Las Vegas for every eight residents.

In Eureka, Nevada, men are forbidden from kissing women.

The Las Vegas Chamber of Commerce, founded in 1911, is the fourth largest Chamber in the United States.

Nevada is the largest gold producing state in the United States. Nevada is second in the world behind South Africa.

Seventeen of the top twenty hotels in the world are located in Las Vegas.

Construction workers on the Hoover Dam in 1933 were treated to a new invention, the hard hat. The hard hat was invented specifically for workers on the Hoover Dam.

Nevada has about 50,000 miles of paved roads.

Did you know that in a standard deck of cards the King of Hearts is the only King without a moustache?

On the average, approximately 230 marriage licenses are issued per day in Las Vegas.

In 1899, the first slot machine was invented by Charles Fey. It was called the Liberty Bell.

The Wynn Casino and the Rio Casino do not have any elevator floors that start with the number four. This is because the number four is not lucky in the Chinese culture.

Carson City, Nevada, is one of the smallest state capitals in the United States.

Many famous people have worked in Nevada. Jack Dempsey was the bartender and the bouncer at the Mispah Hotel and Casino.

Another famous person who worked in Nevada was Wyatt Earp. He maintained law and order in the town of Tonopah, Nevada.

In 1938, saddled horses were banned from inside casinos.

Nevada is the seventh largest state with 110,540 square miles, more than eighty-five percent of the land is federally owned.

Nevada is also famous for not having a state income tax.

48

TOURISTS

N ow that you know a little bit about the history of Las Vegas, let's take a look at the people who flock there to see the shows, wine and dine, sit by the pools, chase the ghosts, and spend their hard earned money. Here's how they break down:

LAS VEGAS VISITOR STATISTICS	
Male visitors	50%
Female visitors	50%
Percentage of USA residents	88%
Singles	14%
Married	79%
Employed	67%
College Graduate	44%
Average Age	49
Race/white	86%
Average Stay	3.5 nights/4.5 days
Food/Drink	$254.49
Shopping	$114.50
Room cost	$ 99.51
Spent on sightseeing	$ 8.31
Spent on shows	$108.87
Visitors Attending Shows	63%

(Updated 11/2007)

A parting shot of the Las Vegas Strip.
Public Domain—courtesy PDPhoto.org.

LOCATION OF LODGING

Strip	73%
Downtown	14%
Boulder Hwy	10%
Other	3%

TRANSPORTATION TO LAS VEGAS

Air	46%
Automobile	43%
Bus	8%
RV	4%

OTEHR STATISTICS

Percent of visitors who gamble	84%
Average # Hours per day	3.4
First Time Visitor	18%
Repeat Visitors	79%
Number Visits past year	2

49

GOT GHOSTS?

So, you've spent the day touring the city, took a dip in the hotel's pool, filled up at the buffet, and lost your rent at the blackjack table. You feel like you've already done and seen everything, but you haven't. If you're ready to see a different side of Las Vegas, including stops at many of the locations discussed in this book, you're ready to take *the* tour.

Two tours you might want to consider are The Haunted Vegas Tour, for the ghost hunters, and The Vegas Mob Tour, for those interested in mob and gangster history. Both tours are the brain children of Robert Allen and are an educational and extremely entertaining way to learn more about Sin City.

You can visit the tour websites to book your outing, or you can save up to fifty percent (if you book four days out) by visiting www.halfpriceshows. com. Don't forget your camera, an open mind, and a jacket.

THE HAUNTED VEGAS TOUR

Celebrity Room Greek Isles Hotel and Casino,
305 Convention Center Drive Las Vegas:
http://www.hauntedvegastours.com/.

This spirited and spooky ghost tour will take you to the haunting grounds of Bugsy Siegel, Liberace, Redd Foxx, and Elvis. Robert Allen now makes it possible to visit such eerie sites by offering a guided tour, featuring Sin City's Darkest Ghostly Secrets. The tour covers such haunted sites as the "Motel of Death," where numerous celebrity deaths have occurred and the former home of a Las Vegas legend whose ghost continues to haunt the place despite numerous attempts to exorcise it.

VEGAS MOB TOUR

Celebrity Room Greek Isles Hotel and Casino,
305 Convention Center Drive Las Vegas:
http://www.vegasmobtour.com/.

The Vegas Mob Tour is a two and a half hour bus tour that reveals the sordid history of Las Vegas. Strange tales of Sin City's colorful past fill the air. Guests learn the truth about the notorious gangster/casino builder Benjamin "Bugsy" Siegel, infamous mob enforcer Tony "The Ant" Spilotro, and casino boss Frank "Lefty" Rosenthal, as well as celebrity deaths, suicides, and many other strange and puzzling Nevada mysteries.

CONCLUSION

Las Vegas is an exciting city to visit with lots to do and to explore. If you go specifically to investigate haunted sites, we hope we've given you some information to help you plot your course.

Keep in mind you might be able to see a mist or apparition while the person standing next to you is completely oblivious to it. Ghosts and spirits usually only appear to sensitive people who are receptive to their presence. *They* decide who will be able to see them; we don't.

Serious ghost hunters usually have vast paranormal knowledge and professional equipment, including, thermometers, electronic light and sound meters, and night vision cameras. The paranormal boom is big business, and authors, advertisers, and "haunted destinations" are raking it in. But not every ghost hunter has fancy tools and devices; even fewer have the knowledge needed to keep themselves safe.

Pay attention to your surroundings; listen to that little voice in your head. If something doesn't feel right to you, it probably isn't. Leave.

It's exciting to get home and find an orb or mist in a photo that you've taken. But do you really want to contact a ghost or spirit? It may sound like fun, but it can be both frightening and dangerous. There really isn't any way to weed out good spirits from bad when you're inviting them to make their presence known. Hypersensitive people are especially vulnerable to negative influences and entities.

Have you ever seen an orb in a photo? What about a strange mist or apparition? Sometimes there's a logical explanation; sometimes not.

An orb describes an unexpected, typically circular object in a photograph. They can result from reflection of light off solid particles, liquid particles, or other foreign material within the camera lens. People often claim that they never saw an orb before they started "ghost hunting:" interestingly, orbs really are captured less frequently in "normal" photo situations. Orbs can be of any color but are typically off white and are usually circular. Yes, it could just be dust particles or a drop of water, and many of them are. While there's no tangible proof to confirm that orbs are spirits, there also is no concrete proof that they aren't.

Did you play with Ouija Boards when you were a kid? You might think of it as a harmless board game, but it can be a portal to the other side. Once you've opened the door, you really have no control over who comes in or if they go out. Don't invite trouble.

It's great fun to ghost hunt, but be respectful wherever you go and shield yourself with a mental white light of protection, a confident and positive attitude, and a prayer. (Of course, remember to never trespass on private property.)

BIBLIOGRAPHY

Amandaquerque, www.squidoo.com.

Barlett, Donald L. and Steele, James B. Howard Hughes: *His Life and Madness*. New York and London: W. W. Norton & Company, Inc., 1979.

Block, Lawrence (editor). *Gangsters, Swindlers, Killers, and Thieves: The Lives and Crimes of Fifty American Villains*. New York: Oxford University Press, Inc., 2004.

Brown, Peter Harry and Broeske, Pat H. *Howard Hughes: The Untold Story*. New York: The Penguin Group/Penguin Books USA, Inc., 1996.

Burbank, Jeff. *Las Vegas Babylon: True Tales of Glitter, Glamour, and Greed*. New York: M. Evans and Company, Inc., 2005.

Chandler, J. D. Frank Sinatra and the Mob. http://www.crimemagazine.com/sinatra.htm.

Churchwell, Sarah. *The Many Lives of Marilyn Monroe*. New York: Metropolitan Books, Henry Holt and Company, 2004.

Cridland, Tim, Weird Las Vegas and Nevada, (Sterling Publishing Company, 2007).

www.erinpavlina.com.

www.funtrivia.com/Redd Foxx.

Fagan, Kevin, *San Francisco Chronicle*, June 17, 2001

Ferrari, Michelle with Ives, Stephen. *Las Vegas: An Unconventional History*. Companion to the PBS American Experience Documentary, New York-Boston: Bulfinch Press (New York-Boston), Time Warner Book Group, 2005.

Fischer, Steve. *When the Mob Ran Vegas: Stories of Money, Mayhem and Murder*. Omaha, Nebraska: Berkline Press, 2005/2006/2007.

Fisher, Kristi and Fisher, Mark. "Seize the Night" website, www.carpenoctem.tv/haunt/nv/.

http://www.geocities.com/welkerlots/carole.htm.

http://www.geocities.com/welkerlots/lights.htm.

www.ghosttowns.com.

www.halfpriceshows.com.

www.hauntedlasvegastours.com

"Haunted Nevada". http://travelwand.com.

Hersh, Burton. *Bobby and J. Edgar: The Historic Face-off Between the Kennedys and J. Edgar Hoover that Transformed America*. New York: Carroll & Graf Publishers, an imprint of Avalon Publishing Group, Inc., 2007.

Herczog, Mary. *Fromm's Las Vegas 2008*. Hoboken, New Jersey, Wiley Publishing, Inc., 2008.

www.insiderviewpoint.com/.

www.insidervlv.com.

Krohn, Katherine E. *Marilyn Monroe: Norma Jeane's Dream.* Minneapolis: Lerner Publications Company, 1997.

www.kvbc.com.

Land, Barbara and Land, Myrick. *A Short History of Las Vegas.* Reno-Las Vegas, Nevada: University of Nevada Press, 1999.

www.lasvegas.citisearch.com

Las Vegas & the Desert. Maspeth, New York: APA Publications/Langtenscheidt Publications, Inc./Discovery Channel, 2003.

"Las Vegas: Garden Ghost?". http://.travel.discovery.com.

Las Vegas: Insight City Guide. Maspeth, New York: APA Publications/ Langenscheidt Publications, Inc./Discovery Channel, 2003.

www.Las Vegas journal.com.

www.Las Vegas Mercury.com.

www.Las Vegas Sun.com, Thu, Jan 10, 2002

www.lasvegassun.com/

Levy, Shawn. *Rat Pack Confidential: Frank, Dean, Sammy, Peter, Joey & the Last Great Showbiz Party.* New York: Doubleday, a division of Bantom Doubleday Dell Publishing Group, Inc., 1998.

www.liberace.org.

Martin, Deana with Holden, Wendy. *Memories Are Made Of This: Dean Martin Through His Daughter's Eyes.* New York: Harmony Books, 2004.

Mitchell, Deborah Arizona Travel by, www.suite101.com

Mobsters and Gangsters: Organized Crime in America from Al Capone to Tony Soprano. Life Books.

www.neonmusesum.org.

www.onlinenevada.org.

Pahler, Stanley W. *Las Vegas: As It Began-As It Grew.* Las Vegas: Nevada Publications, 1971.

Randisi, Robert J. *Luck Be a Lady, Don't Die: A Rat Pack Mystery.* New York: Thomas Dunne Booke/St. Martin's Minotaur, 2007.

Randisi, Robert J. *Everybody Kills Somebody Sometime: A Rat Pack Mystery.* New York: Thomas Dunne Books/St. Martin's Minotaur, 2006.

Reppetto, Thomas. *American Mafia: A History of Its Rise to Power.* New York: a John Macrae Book, Henry Holt and Company, 2004.

Server, Lee. *Ava Gardner: Love Is Nothing.* New York: St. Martin's Press, 2006.

Smith, John L. "The First 100: Part II: Resort Rising: Benjamin Siegel". *Las Vegas Review-Journal*, www.1st100.com.

Summers, Anthony and Swan, Robbyn. *Sinatra: The Life*. New York: Alfred A. Knopf, 2005.

Weiser, Kathy. http://www.LegendsofAmerica.com/NV-GoldfieldHotel.html.

"Flamingo Las Vegas". http://.en.wikipedia.org/wiki/Flamingo_Las_Vegas.

"Benjamin Bugsy Siegel". www.RoadsideAmerica.com.

"Bugsy Siegel Memorial". www.RoadsideAmerica.com.

"Frank Sinatra". http://en.wikipedia.org/wiki/Frank_Sinatra.

"Howard Hughes". http://en.wikipedia.org/wiki/Howard_Hughes.

"Howard Hughes". http://famoustexans.com/howardhughes.htm.

"Tina Sinatra: Mob Ties Aided JFK". http://www.cbsnews.com/stories/2000/10/05/60minutes/main23890.shtml.

www.vegas.com.

"Vegas". www.crimelibrary.com. Courtroom Television Network, LLC, A Time Warner Company, 2007.

"Gangsters—Bugsy Siegel". www.bugsysclub.com.

"Bugsy Siegel Biography". www.freeinfosociety.com.

"Fire Department-MGM". www.fire.co.clark.nv.us.

"Marilyn Monroe". http://www.imdb.com/name/nm0000054/bio.

"MGM Fire—Parts 1-6". www.knpr.org/lvirmgn.cfm.

"The MGM Grand Hotel Fire Investigation Report". http://.co.clrk.nv.us/fire/ccfd__mgm.htm.

http://www.murphsplace.com/lombard/end.html.

"A Byte Out of History: The Case of the Disappearing Diamond". Federal Bureau of Investigation Headline Archives. www.fbi.gov/diamond_byte111706.htm.

"Nevada's Haunted Hotspots". www.carpenoctem.tv/haunt/nv. c. 2000 CarpeNoctem.

www.people.com.

Powers, Ashley, "Preserving a Beloved Watering Hole," Los Angeles Times, Sunday, April 13, 2008.

www.reddfoxx.com.

www.shadowlands.net/places/nevada.htm.

www.Strangeusa.com.

"Top Haunted Spots," http://lasvegas.citysearch.com/roundup/40468.

Weiser, Katy, Legends of America, updated June, 2008.

www.Wikipedia.com.